古武道
棒術

Bo Jutsu Kobudo
Calligraphy written by T. Hokama

WARNING

The techniques described in this book and the techniques of any martial art are dangerous. You must train under the supervision of an expert. Please use caution when handling any weapons and consult a qualified teacher. Please use restraint when practicing techniques described in this book. Neither the author nor the publishers of this book are responsible for the results of your choice to practice these techniques. Please respect the law and order of your country.

Helmut Kogel

KOBUDO BO-JUTSU

Technique – Training – Katas

Meyer & Meyer Sport

British Library Cataloguing in Publication Data
A catalogue record for this book is available from the British Library

Kobudo – Bo-Jutsu
Helmut Kogel
Oxford: Meyer & Meyer Sport (UK) Ltd., 2006
ISBN-10: 1-84126-172-6
ISBN-13: 978-1-84126-172-0

© 2006 by Meyer & Meyer Sport (UK) Ltd.
Aachen, Adelaide, Auckland, Budapest, Graz, Johannesburg,
New York, Olten (CH), Oxford, Singapore, Toronto
Member of the World
Sports Publishers' Association (WSPA)
www.w-s-p-a.org
Printed and bound by: TZ Verlag, Germany
ISBN-10: 1-84126-172-6
ISBN-13: 978-1-84126-172-0
E-Mail: verlag@m-m-sports.com
www.m-m-sports.com

CONTENTS

Foreword by Tetsuhiro Hokama
(Nishihara, Okinawa, June 23, 2004)

Professor Helmut Kogel M.D. is an excellent Karate and Kobojutsu teacher. I would like to place emphasis on the specific feature that he is a professor of medicine and a Karate teacher at the same time. He has also done research on Chinese Kenpo and Bubishi. The study and the comprehension of Bubishi, the literary and historical basis of Karate, are an indispensable prerequisite for every Karateka. In his book Professor Kogel describes his view of Okinawan Karate or rather as we say – Kobujutsu.

The book is divided into a general part and a special part. It contains numerous pictures, photos and graphics, which give us an excellent insight into the Okinawan martial art. The clear description of Bojutsu and its similarity to Karate and the different Karate techniques is an important contribution to the preservation of our cultural heritage.

The new and graphic presentation of traditional Bo-Katas in this book is clearly arranged and understandable for every Karateka. To my mind this is one of the most remarkable features of this monograph. The compilation of the numerous Katas has doubtless been one of the most difficult and time-consuming tasks for the author. Moreover, I want to place emphasis on chapters such as "Uke Kata versus Seme Kata", "Basic Fighting Exercises" and "Katas", because in this form they have not been dealt with so far.

That is why I can particularly recommend the careful study of this textbook to everyone who has an interest in martial arts.

Tetsuhiro Hokama Hanshi, 9th Dan Gojuryu Karatedo, PhD mult.
President of the Gojuryu Kenshikai Federation
Curator of the Okinawan Karate Museum
Technical consultant of the Karatedo Kenyukai Japan
Contract Researcher of Okinawa Cultural Assets
Member of the Planning Committee of the Okinawan Kobudo World Championship
Member of the Educational Committee of Nishihara Okinawa (Japan)

Already in 1952, Sensei Hokama began learning the fundamentals of Okinawa Karate from his grandfather Tokuyama Seiken, an expert in Okinawan Martial Arts. In 1961 Hokama began with the training of Gojuryu under the Masters Higa Seiko and Fukushi Seiko. He practiced Kobudo under Matayoshi Shinpo. He gave lectures on physical education at Ryukyu University and on Kobudo and Karate at Kinki University Toyooka Junior College. He has won many international awards, e.g. in 1999 the Okinawan Cultural Award. Moreover, he was nominated for the title "preserver of cultural heritage". International seminars and courses in the U.S.A., Great Britain, France, Italy, Canada, Hong Kong, the Philippines, South Africa, Finland, Mexico, Taiwan, Vatican City, Switzerland and Sweden helped him to get a high repute and to achieve fame at home and abroad.

Foreword by Hans-Dieter Rauscher (Freiburg, Germany, September 3, 2004)

It gives me a lot of pleasure and it is a matter of personal concern to recommend the careful study of this Bo-Jutsu textbook by Professor Helmut Kogel M.D. to the great number of people all over the world who have an interest in Kobudo. For decades, Professor Helmut Kogel has intensively concerned himself with the martial art of Budo. By continuous theoretical and practical studies, scientific research and the attendance of countless seminars on martial arts at home and abroad, he has acquired an excellent knowledge in various disciplines such as Nihon-Jujutsu, Karate-Do, Bo-Jutsu, Tonfa, Sai, Arnis, and others.

Because of his great knowledge he became a renowned member of the DAKO (German Martial Arts Organisation) and thus became acquainted with the Kokusai-Budoin-IMAF (International Martial Arts Federation), the oldest Japanese International Federation. Owing to his qualifications, the rare Budo title "Renshi", the Japanese instructor licences and offices, such as the office of regional director were conferred on him by the Kokusai-Budoin-IMAF. Thus he could intensify his strong commitment to the spread of the Budo art.

On numerous training and study trips to the IMAF-Budo-Headquarters in Tokyo organized by Hans-D. Rauscher for European Budokas, Professor Kogel increased his background knowledge and extended his research. In Tokyo he attended further training courses supervised by the most important Japanese Grand Masters. Training and study trips to the Grand Masters on Okinawa completed his in-depth knowledge and his qualification. He became a great Budo Master and teacher. In the knowledge that in this day and age, Budo is of great importance to man, Professor Helmut Kogel has—in addition to his responsible position as a consultant surgeon—managed to direct a renowned Budo dojo and to be a successful member of the leading teaching staff of great international IMAF-DAKO seminars on martial arts.

Over and over again, his extraordinarily pedagogical talent, his great insight into human nature and his teaching experience enable him at these specific classes to give interesting and valuable lessons, which motivate his students and make them show renewed enthusiasm for Budo. This textbook makes an outstanding contribution and addition to an in-depth study of Budo for all his students and, of course, for all the friends of Budo. A textbook like this one is of great benefit to

Budokas of all disciplines, likewise for Karatekas and for Jujitsukas, who want to do research on Budo more effectively and who want to work interdisciplinarily in order to gain greater insight into Budo. Everyone who practices several martial arts knows how helpful and useful it is for the main martial art to study the connection between the various disciplines as well as the historical and technical developments.

An in-depth knowledge of the general connection between the Budo martial arts will often enable the student to completely understand the specific features of his main martial art. The careful study of Bo-Jutsu is an important pillar and prerequisite of a clear understanding of the Budo martial arts. Many traditional Karate-Do-Kata, i.e. those containing Bo elements, can only be inferred after having studied authentic Bo-Jutsu.

Bo-Jutsu is eminently suitable for practical demonstrations of Kumite with Tonfa, Sai, Kama or Tanbo. It is little-known that the principles of Bo are also particularly suitable for self-defense, e.g. with a leather belt or a handbag. In Europe, Bo-Jutsu has a particularly long tradition in the DAKO and the IMAF. Already in the seventies, masters of the DAKO and the IMAF organized the first international Kata and Kumite championships in Germany. The competitions have gone very well. Just the other day, the IMAF Germany/DAKO organized the 28th German Championships. The form of free fight in Bo-Jutsu, which many Masters have at their command at a high level, is physically and mentally a top performance, even if the competitors wear protective clothing. It is true, that the Bo-Jutsu fight without any form of protection, which is not practiced in tournaments, requires maximum discipline, body control and perfect technique. Finally, I once more want to recommend the Kobudo art of Bo-Jutsu as an interesting topic of Budo research and as a personal challenge to the new and old friends of Bo-Jutsu.

It is a real stroke of luck for all friends of Bo-Jutsu that the author of this new Bo-Jutsu textbook, Professor Helmut Kogel, is an extraordinarily competent, well-informed and renowned expert on Budo especially on Kobudo. He is an expert of high repute at home and abroad.

H. D. Rauscher
President of the IMAF (Kokusai Budoin) Europe
DAKO chief instructor
8th Dan Karatedo Hanshi (IMAF Japan)
7th Dan Bo-Jutsu
6th Dan Kobudo Kyoshi (IMAF Japan)
7th Dan Iaido Kyoshi (IMAF Japan)
8th Antas Arnis

H.-D. Rauscher is a founder member of the German Karate Federation (DKB), which is the oldest German Karate Federation. He is 8th Dan Hanshi Karate Do IMAF Japan. He was the first European, on whom the title Hanshi was conferred by the Budo world headquarters IMAF Japan. He has practiced Budo for more than 50 years, Judo and Jujitsu from childhood, Bo-Jutsu (7th Dan) and Kobudo (6th Dan Kyoshi IMAF Japan) for more than 40 years. After practicing sword arts for several decades, he was awarded the 7th Dan Kyoshi in Japan and as one of European IAIDO sword Masters qualified with the highest degree. For several decades he has intensively studied the Chinese martial arts and the Philippine Arnis-Eskrima stick fighting arts. Thus he has been able to compare the principles of martial arts of different countries more effectively. He is one of the five Europeans to receive the high Japanese award Budo-Koro-Sho and up to now he is the only non-Japanese on whom the great award Budo-Koseki-Sho was conferred by the IMAF headquarters Japan.

Foreword by Shizuya Sato

T he aim of Kokusai Budoin, IMAF since its foundation was to support and practice various martial arts of traditional Japanese Budo. One other principle is to look for cultural exchange and friendship all over the world in order to contribute to peace in different countries.

Martial arts include ancient (ko-ryu) and modern styles (gendai-ryu). In Japan Bujutsu contains military training such as Ken Jutsu (sword), So-Jutsu (spear), Kyu-Jutsu (Archery) and Kumi-Jutsu (grappling).

The long period of peace during the Edo period (1600-1867) led to a change of martial arts. The different budo arts became also popular for common people. The prohibition of arms enhanced the development of unarmed combat techniques. The change of the government from a feudal system to a constitutional monarchy (1898) caused a further change in Budo arts.

The intention of martial arts now reflected more the cultural, mental and physical training and sporting aspects of life. Many old styles of the Edo period remained unchanged called Japanese "Kobudo", that consists of Iaido (ancient styles), Naginata-do, Jodo and others.

Modern Budo (Gendai Budo) developed in the Meiji period (1867-1912). Different styles and sytems have been inaugurated. During the Taisho period (1912-1926), Karate Do and Okinawa Kobudo have been introduced from the Ryukyu islands and completed the system of Japanese Martial arts. Further influences in Okinawan martial arts have also caused further intensive changes in armed and unarmed disciplines.

It is a great pleasure that one of our members of Kokusai Budoin IMAF Professor Helmut Kogel M.D. has written a book about Bo-Jutsu – one of the important Kobudo disciplines.

He has built bridges between the traditions of Kobudo of the Japanese mainland and the Okinawan Kobudo. His book gives a profound insight into the basics of Bo-Jutsu. His new graphical technique showing traditional Bo-Katas will help interested peolple all over the world to study and train the old art of Bo-Jutsu.

His book will contribute to our intention to recognize and support numerous ancient styles and traditions of Japanese Budo, as an heritage of Japan's culture.

Shizuya Sato

Professor Shizuya Sato
Chief Director Kokusai Budoin, IMAF
10th Dan Nihon Jujutsu, Hanshi
9th Dan Judo, Hanshi
Headquarters Tokyo, December 25, 2004

PREFACE

This book, here appearing in its first edition, deals with the martial art of the long stick, the so-called Bo-Jutsu. Bo-Jutsu is one part of the Kobudo system which originates from the islands of Okinawa. My aim is to introduce beginners to different fighting techniques with simple combinations and likewise, I want to give advanced students new insights into difficult exercises. Furthermore, the book provides a comprehensive overview of the history of Kobudo and its development.

Important details of careful planning and preparation of training for advanced students and teachers will be discussed and a systematic survey of different techniques for absolute beginners as well as for advanced students will be given. The main intention of the book is to provide a clear presentation of the Kobudo techniques both at a basic level and of traditional Kobudo Katas.

Similar to the detailed recipes of a cookbook, this book will help students and teachers of Bo-Jutsu to achieve their aims. The chapter "Traditional Katas" will be of special interest to experts, above all, because in most English and German books you can only find diagrams of Katas like Sushi no Kon sho and Sakugawa no Kon. In this book you will find a lot of clear diagrams of numerous different Katas. Of course, this book cannot take the place of qualified guidance by experts such as advanced black belt holders.

I am particularly grateful to many of my teachers, who have guided and instructed me during the last decades in Karate-Do, Jujutsu, Kobudo, and in Combat Arnis. I am indebted to H. D. Rauscher, 8th Dan Karate Hanshi, 7th Dan Kobudo Kyoshi, 6th Dan Iaido Renshi, 8th Antas Arnis and others, to I. Higushi, 9th Dan Karate

Hanshi, 7th Dan Kobudo Kyoshi, and to K.Sakai, 9th Dan Karate Hanshi, 8th Dan Kempo Hanshi. I am obliged to Prof. S. Sato, 10th Dan Nihon Jujutsu Hanshi, 9th Dan Judo Hanshi, and to H. Kanazawa, 10th Dan Karate Hanshi and more. My special gratitude to Tetsuhiro Hokama Ph.D., 9th Dan Karate/Kobudo Hanshi, who gave me important insights into original Okinawan Kobudo.

I hope this book will offer an easy approach to the martial art of Bo-Jutsu. Additional literature on history, philosophical background, and theories of training and medical aspects in sports, about Kyusho (vital points) and about Japanese medical arts (acupressure, Kuatsu) should be studied.

Lippstadt, Germany, May 2005

Prof. Dr. med. H. Kogel
4th Dan Shotokan Karate Renshi
4th Dan Kobudo
1st Dan Nihon Jujusu
1st Dan Antas Arnis 1. Dan Nihon Jujusu
1. Antas Arnis

A GENERAL PART

1   OKINAWA (Ryu Kyu)

The Ryu Kyu Islands chain (Jap. *Ryukyu-retto* or *Nansei-shot*) is an archipelago which stretches between Kyushu and Taiwan. The archipelago is composed of three principal groups: they are, from north to south, the Amami Islands (part of Kagoshima Prefecture), the Okinawa Islands, and the Sakishima Islands, which include the Miyako and Yaeyama groups (both part of Okinawa Prefecture). The islands are the exposed tops of submarine mountains and are of volcanic or coral origin. They cover a total area of approx.,1,850 sq. miles (4,790 sq km) with a total land area of approx. 922 sq. miles (2,245 sq. km).

Continuous human habitation may be traced to about 4,000 years ago. The two northern island groups (Amami and Okinawa) show evidence of southward migration from Kyushu (Jomon Period 13,000 BC to 300 BC), whereas in the southern island groups (Miyako and Yaeyama) evidence points to Melanesian cultural strains from the south. The largest and most important of the Okinawa Islands is Okinawa. It is a long, narrow, irregularly shaped island of volcanic origin with coral formations in the southern part. It covers an area of approx. 454 square miles (1,176 sq km). At present, it has a population of approx. 1,300,000 people. About eighty percent of the population live in an area in or around the cities of Naha and Okinawa. Naha is the largest city and chief port.

Okinawa is the nucleus of the Okinawa Prefecture, Japan's most south westerly prefecture. The Okinawa Prefecture is located southwest of mainland Japan, at 24 degrees to 27 degrees north and 122 degrees to 128 degrees 30' east. The Prefecture consists of 161 islands (44 inhabited and 117 uninhabited islands), and those islands span 1,000 kilometers from east to west and 400 kilometers from north to south. The Prefecture is in the subtropical climate zone and is found in the same latitude as the other famous beach resort destinations such as Hawaii, Florida, and the Bahamas. The relatively constant warm temperatures and frequent rainfall of the subtropical zone keep the islands green throughout the year. It is a southern paradise where colorful flowers of the subtropics such as hibiscus bloom the year-round.

The outer circle of the Okinawa prefectural symbol represents the ocean. The white circle symbolizes a peace-loving Okinawa and the inner circle symbolizes a globally developing Okinawa. In short, the emblem symbolizes "Ocean", "Peace", and "Development."

2 THE DEVELOPMENT OF KOBUJUTSU (Kobudo)

Okinawa's location as one of the islands in the Ryu Kyu Archipelago in the Pacific Ocean was the main reason for the development of a special kind of martial art, which was different from Chinese and Japanese martial arts. The origins of the Okinawan form of martial art are not quite clear, but were most likely born from the synthesis of an external style of martial art brought from China and native Okinawan fighting techniques. According to a 1,000-year-old tradition, it was at the Shaolin monastery that the founder of Zen Buddhism, the 6th-century monk Boddhidharma (Daruma Daishi in Japanese), preached and meditated until his death. Boddhidharma or Ta Mo (as he was called by the Chinese) helped the Shaolin monks to develop a system of self-defence that became known throughout the world as Kung Fu. They used long wooden poles, spears and Sais as weapons to defend the monastery against bandits and other enemies.

The first Sho family line, the so-called Sho Hashi's lineage, ended with the 7th King, Sho Toku. Then Kanamura became King Sho En in 1470 and started the second Sho family line. The third king of the second Sho line King Sho Shin established centralism, a social ranking system, and trade with the Chinese Ming Dynasty. Because of the prosperous Ryu Kyu culture through associations with Japan, China and Southeast Asia, this era is known as the so called "golden Era of the Ryu Kyu Dynasty". When King Sho Shin of the Ryu Kyu Kingdom made the wearing of swords and possession of weapons illegal throughout the Ryukyu Kingdom, the traditional Okinawan weapons assumed importance. As the ban on weapons continued for many years the Okinawans began to develop a special kind of self-defence with bare hands (Okinawa Te) and with everyday objects such as the Tonfa (originally a farming implement used as a handle to turn the millstone), the Bo (a long wooden staff), the Nunchaku (originally a flail), the Kama (a wooden handle with a sharpened metal blade used to harvest rice, a small scythe), the Kai also called Aku or Eiku (originally an oar used by the Okinawan fishermen), the Sai (originally a farming implement used to measure the distance between the seeds), and many others.

In 1609, the Satsuma clan of southern Japan took possession of Okinawa. After the Japanese conquest, the main objective of the Okinawans was to put up strong resistance against the arbitrary rule and despotism of the Samurai and marauding bandits. As the previous ban on import, possession and use of weapons was reinforced, the Okinawan martial arts, with the help of everyday objects and bare or "empty" hands, reached their zenith. Kobujutsu – as it was formerly called – embraced different techniques of martial arts both with and without weapons for the purpose of self-defence. For the purpose of keeping it hidden from the Japanese invaders, training in Kobujutsu took place and was shrouded in absolute secrecy. In order to achieve a perfect choreography of the many movements, they were normally practiced in unique Katas. Many of these choreographed movements were incorporated in the traditional Okinawan dances (Odori) in order to preserve essential elements in an unobtrusive way. The training methods, techniques, and Katas were passed down by verbal instruction and the old, almost secretive, face-to-face teaching methods from instructors to pupils. There were only a few written instructions. During the invasion of Okinawa at the end of World War II, many of these rare sources went up in flames and were lost forever. That is why it is very hard for contemporary practitioners to know what is traditional, what has been changed, and what has been lost.

It was not before the end of the 19th or the beginning of the 20th century that the techniques without weapons (Okinawa-Te) were separated from the techniques with weapons. For the ancient weapon arts, this separation gave birth to the Okinawan Kobudo, which means as much as the "old" or "little" Budo. The Okinawan Kobudo is different from the Japanese Kobudo, because only everyday objects have been turned into weapons. The typical weapons of the Japanese Samurais such as Jaido (swords), Naginata (halberds), Kyudo (archery) and many more traditional Japanese weapons are not used in the Okinawan Kobudo. Many of the traditional Kobujutsu techniques have been preserved in the traditional Katas and Okinawan dances (Odori).

Okinawan Drum Dancers at a Gala Dinner in Ginowan City

Kobudo Weapons in the Karate Museum of Tetsuhiro Hokama in Nishihara City on Okinawa

3   KOBUDO MASTERS AND THEIR STYLES

V arious Karate styles without weapons were growing in popularity and spread all over the world, because they — above all else — were suitable for national and international championships; however, such was not the case with Kobudo. There are comparatively few qualified Kobudo dojos in the martial arts world outside of Japan. Perhaps the main reason for the slow spread of Kobudo is the fact that — in contrast to Karate and judo — for many years there have not been any chances to hold tournaments and competitions.

More recently, the traditional purpose of self-defense of some Okinawan weapons has again assumed importance, such as Tonfa techniques for security forces. Irrespective of the Okinawan weapons, the Filipino martial art Arnis enjoys great popularity among security forces and even secret services all over the world. The short rattan stick, the main weapon of Arnis, can be used for precise and quick techniques. Furthermore, the technique of single stick fighting (the most common system in Arnis) can easily be applied to everyday objects, such as for example umbrellas or newspapers.

In the last century, numerous Okinawan masters had the merit of finding and applying themselves to Kobudo. So, many dojos were founded, which –- in this book — can only be dealt with in extracts. I want to confine myself to the Bo staff as the Kobudo weapon.

YAMANI RYU

It is possible that a lot of this style has been lost. The founder was Chinen Yamane Masami (1898-1976). Different influences of various masters played a role in this connection. Typical of Yamani Ryu is that the centrifugal forces of the rotation of the Bo are intentionally utilized. Comparable to turning pirouettes, the radius is reduced by drawing hands and arms closer too the body. Thus the angular acceleration and speed is essentially increased (angular momentum conservation law: $w_2 = w_1(r_1^2/r_2^2)$ It is important for this style to use circular movements or parts of circles and ellipses and to shorten the axis of the arms holding the Bo and the steps of the gliding movements (Suri Ashi) simultaneously.

One of the contemporary Grand Masters is Sensei Toshihiro Oshiro, who has a name for his international courses and seminars and video productions.

Honshin Ryu

Another style is Honshin Ryu. It was founded by Sensei Miyagi Masakatzu. At the bottom of this style lies an old Karate style, "Uechi-Ryu". It was on the basis of this style that Miyagi Chojun built his own dojo after practising Kobudo under the tutelage of several old Senseis.

Ryukyu Kobudo

Ryukyu Kobudo can be traced back to Jabiku Moden (1882-1945) and Taira Shinken (1897-1970). Contemporary representatives of this style were Inoe Motukatsu and Akamine Eiko. Currently, central dojos for Ryukyu Kobudo are on Japan's Mainland.

Ufu-Chiku-Kobudo

According to W. Lind, Ufu-Chiku-Kobudo is a relatively modern style, which originates from Sensei Kanagusuku Sanda and Sensei Kina Shosai (1883-1981). Ufu-Chiku-Kobudo is not widely spread.

Matayoshi Kobudo

Matayoshi Shoshi Kobudo is another style which was essentially influenced by its representatives Matayoshi Shinkô (1888-1947) and Matayoshi Shinpo (1923-1997). Shinpo's father, Matayoshi Shinkô, studied different martial arts in China and occupied himself with medical topics (acupuncture, botany). Typical of this style is a relatively high standing position, which makes quick, flexible and supple movements possible.

Another characteristic feature of this style is that the Bo staff is not directed to the costal arch but to the periphery of the upper arm, while you are striking a lateral blow to the upper level (Yoko Uchi). Among others, contemporary representatives of this Kobudo style are e.g. Yoshiaki Gakiya (8th Dan Kyoshi), who has his own association, the Okinawa-Kobudo-Doushi Rensai-Kai, and Tetsuhiro Hokama (9th Dan Hanshi), who is president of Okinawa-Goju-Ryu Kenshi-Kai-Karate/ Kobudo, and who has founded a Karate museum in Nishihara (Okinawa) in 1987.

His Karate originates from Chojun Miyagi, Seiko Higa and Seiko Fukushi, his Kobudo from Shinpo Matayoshi, Seiko Higa and Seiken Tokuyama. He began to train Karate under the supervision of his grandfather Seiken Tokuyama, who was the neighbor of Mr. Ufugusuku near Shuri Castle in Naha City. Ufugusuku (nickname Oshiro) was a well known Bo-Jutsu expert and created the Kata Ufugusuku no Kun (see the chapter about Katas).

Tetsuhiro Hokama made different videos and he wrote 10 books about Karate, two in English. One book, which he wrote nearly 20 years ago, deals with Bubishi. This book was a bestseller in Japan. McCarthy took this text as a basis for his own book (Bubishi: The Secret of Karate). Hokama was informed about Bubishi by his teacher Seiko Higa.

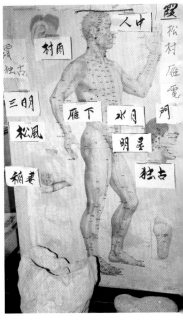

Table of Acupuncture for Application of Kyusho in the Karate Museum of Tetsuhiro Hokama

Another style's Grand Master of modern times is Fumino Demura, whose books and video films essentially helped to spread Kobudo all over the world. A greater number of Grand Masters could be mentioned, but that would be beyond the scope of this book.

The Kobudo dojos of Japan's Mainland differ greatly from Okinawan Kobudo in technique, weapons and Katas. There are some associations which apply themselves to Kobudo by different measures. IMAF (Kokusai Budoin, International Martial Arts Federation) comprises various styles, which are looked after by T. Kawabata (10th Dan Hanshi), I. Higushi (9th Dan Shotokan Karate Hanshi, 7th Dan Kobudo Kyoshi) and K. Sakai (9th Dan Wado Ryu Karate Hanshi, 8th Dan Kempo Hanshi) and others.

Kazuo Sakai
10th Dan Karate Hanshi
8th Dan Kempo Hanshi
9th Dan Kobudo Hanshi

Ikiu Higushi
9th Dan Karate Hanshi
7th Dan Kobudo Kyoshi on the left
    Tenori Nobetzu
9th Dan Karate Hanshi, middle,
    and the author on the right

The objectives of the Grand Masters are not only the promotion of the techniques of Japanese Martial Arts, but also the maintenance of cultural traditions, the establishment of contact between different cultures and the responsible development of the mind and bodies of the students.

Figuratively speaking, the following quotation expresses the central idea of these objectives:

> "The commander-in-chief represents the virtues of wisdom,
> honesty, benevolence, courage and strictness."
>
> Sunzi – The Art of War

4 THE DISTINCTIVE FEATURES OF DIFFERENT FORMS OF THE BO STAFF

The conventional long staffs (Bo) are 1.82 meters long. In most cases, it is used as a round staff (Maru Bo), but there are also quadrangular (Kaku Bo), hexagonal (Rokkuku Bo) and octagonal (Hakkaku Bo) staffs. Furthermore, there are special forms made of bamboo canes. They must be freshly cut down, because bamboo normally splinters into pieces if used in action. Others are made of rattan, which is extremely light and robust. Even staffs made of iron are used.

Further developments or modifications of the Bo with the same length of 1.82 meters are spears (Yari), halberds (Naginata) oars (called Eku, Kai or Oar). The weapons mentioned last are listed in connection with Bo-Jutsu, because the techniques are similar and should be practiced together with Bo-Jutsu. Further forms are the shorter Yon-shaku-Bo or the longer Kyu-shaku Bo, which is used according to the disposition of the student and dependent on height and constitution.

The standard Bo is the Roku shaku Bo. It is conical at both ends. At the middle it is about 3 centimeters in diameter; both its ends are about 2.5 centimeters. These special forms offer decisive advantages. The transfer of the greatest weight to the middle of the Bo guarantees an optimum balance when using it. In addition to this, the Bo is more robust and solid and does not break so easily.

Usually, the Bo is made of the wood of dark or light Japanese oak trees, which gives it a high degree of solidity. The angular forms of the Bo are more difficult to hold with your hands and to use, but the blow with the edges has a much greater effect (the energy of the pressure is greater if the surface is smaller (because thrust force = F/A (force/area)).

That means, the smaller the area, the larger the thrust force. Other forms such as Tanbo (about 25 centimeters), Hanbo (92-100 centimeters), Jo (130 centimeters) have different purposes and applications. That is why the differences in range (radius of action), maximum acceleration and speed are intelligible. The short Filipino rattan stick (Arnis, Escrima, Kali) has – because of its light weight –

specific features, which make lightning actions possible. The maximum speed at the top of the stick can be as high as 150 kilometers per hour. This speed gives the stick a lot of strength and energy.

The Japanese long stick is much slower, but has a greater range. That makes it possible to keep the enemy more effectively at a distance. But weight and substance of the long stick compensate for the lower speed. Thus enough energy is set free when the Bo hits a surface. In hand-to-hand combat and at medium distance the long stick is definitely inferior to the short stick.

In a fight, the advantages of a Bo, range and weight, should be utilized. That is why big circular and elliptical movements, which make use of the rotation impulse, are in the foreground. The special features will be explained in detail in the Chapter "Basic Principles of Tactics".

Nothing at all – beginning with weapons – should be one-sidedly preferred; relying too much on one thing simply means that you are making it useless.
Miyamoto Musashi

5   THE SYSTEM OF MOVEMENTS IN KOBUDO

Generally speaking, the control over the system of movements and a special feeling for a natural movement, which is tactically correctly adapted to the particular situation, are of essential importance for all martial arts. This includes that careful consideration should be given to the aspects of distance (Mai), the utilization of direction (angle) for diverting the energy (Tai Sabaki) and the utilization of one's own acceleration by drawing back the hand and hip. One essential element of Kobudo is that the weapon and the body form a unity (Ken-tai-ichi-jo).

This defining characteristic does not only require that every movement has to be powerful and accurate, but also that the combination of movements have to differ in some details according to the type of weapon and even to the length of the staff. Looking at the issue only superficially, one might be inclined to believe that this cannot be so difficult, but a feeling for movement means control over the three dimensions of space (height, length, width).

At a time when computers more and more dominate the every day life of our children and adolescents, you have to realize that the feeling for a three-dimensional space gets more and more lost. This becomes evident when in a test, adolescents are scarcely capable of going steadily backwards. Every Karate student and instructor is aware of the phenomenon that coordination gets lost while going backwards. Simple combinations, which can be trained almost without any problems while going forward, do not function properly any longer if moving backwards. It calls for a great effort and long training until these problems of coordination have been overcome.

It is a basic principle of Karate that the combinations and techniques must function perfectly and automatically in all directions. You must practice them very often until you are able to do them blindfold. Especially in a free fight, lack of co-ordination becomes obvious. Students often do not successfully avoid contact by stepping sideways or backwards if they are attacked. That is why sometimes defensive or counter techniques appear awkward, heavy and little effective. Furthermore, people forget far too often that time is an important factor in movement in space. Timing and speed are of great importance to movement in space and they are of paramount importance to the effect and success of the applied techniques. In the case of a hard and effective attack by the opponent, time for a counterattack can be gained by changing the angle in the space, or even by using a weak defensive technique (e.g. Nagashi Uke). That means it is important for the instructor to include the factor of time in the system of movement and tactics.

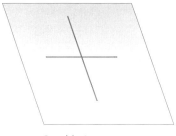

Graphic 1

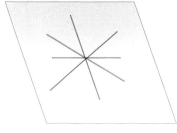

Graphic 2

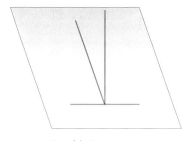

Graphic 3

DEGREES of FREEDOM of the MOVEMENT

In principle, the movements can be directed forward, backwards or sideways. Miyamoto Musashi, a famous Japanese sword fighter (1584-1645) described in his book of the five circles (original title: Gorin-No-Sho) that height is another possible direction for the movement. This is mostly forgotten. By that it means dodging an attack by ducking down. To simplify matters, only a few diagrams are used to illustrate potential directions of movements in the case of attack or defense. They are drawn as different lines on the ground.

This most simple graphic illustrates the directions forward, backwards, to the left side, and to the right side by two crossing lines which make a 90° angle.

A further development is a diagram which incorporates a bisected 45° angle.

Musashi's diagram incorporates height, but makes only use of lines which illustrate a forward or backward movement and to the left side or to the right side.

In Kobudo, even more than in Karate, the 45° movement is mainly theoretical. In practice, there is no clear dividing line between sideways movements. The distance from the opponent determines the angle and thus the direction of the movement. Standing at the correct reach (Mai) is absolutely essential to have success with one or the other technique. The very special difficulty with Kobudo is that you have to form a unified whole with your weapon, that means to develop a feeling for distance.

It is easy to understand how important it is to take these principles into consideration. If someone tries to strike a blow with an axe or a sword at your head, it will be no use blocking the attack in a straight line with Morote Uke (an upward double block) even if a robust oak staff were used. It would be cut or splintered and the attacked person's head would be hit.

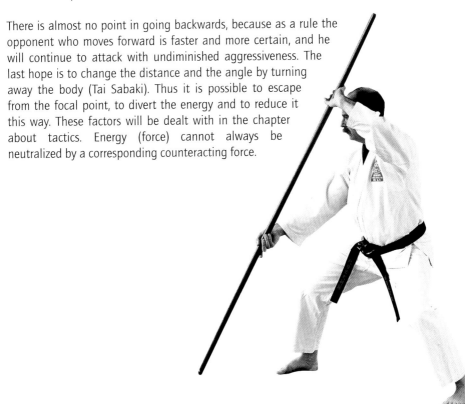

There is almost no point in going backwards, because as a rule the opponent who moves forward is faster and more certain, and he will continue to attack with undiminished aggressiveness. The last hope is to change the distance and the angle by turning away the body (Tai Sabaki). Thus it is possible to escape from the focal point, to divert the energy and to reduce it this way. These factors will be dealt with in the chapter about tactics. Energy (force) cannot always be neutralized by a corresponding counteracting force.

6 BASIC PRINCIPLES OF TACTICS

ZANSHIN

What is special about martial arts is the fact that readiness for an attack and great powers of concentration are always essential, even if you are in a situation where an attack is seemingly improbable. Thus you can avoid being taken and defeated by a surprise attack. That is why it is an important prerequisite to maintain good eye contact with your opponent(s) and avoid being distracted by irrelevant details. If you practice Jaido (swords arts) you should look through your opponent at an imaginary point which is about six meters away. Thus you keep track and can react quickly to several opponents. That is why it is wrong to stare at the opponent's weapon in Kobudo, because it is not his weapon which takes the initiative but he himself, who holds the weapon. Your opponent's body language tells you the beginning of an attack much earlier than the movement of his weapon. If you stare at his weapon, it will be too late for a reaction. The faster the weapon is the more important is this tactical basic principle. This applies to the short stick, knife and especially to Nunchaku. Nobody would get the idea to dodge a bullet. In such a case, if you can possibly manage it, you would take cover before being shot at. Eye contact is of great importance to create an effect of psychological superiority over the opponent. Whoever looks at the ground has already been defeated. Readiness for an attack, however, does not mean body (muscle) tension; otherwise you would start too slowly. You have to remain flexible and supple to be ready to start at the right moment and to land a blow. It is not until the final stage of the blow that the maximum tension (Kime) must have been built up.

SEN NO SEN

With regard to parrying an attack there are alternative methods of perfect timing. One of them is the principle of Sen no Sen. This principle simply means that you head off your opponent before he can complete his attack. The possibilities of Sen no Sen are not limited to starting earlier than or at the same moment as your opponent's attack. Moreover, you can change the angle between you and your opponent in order to make him miss you. You can duck; thus you sneak out of the focus of the attack and instead, you can successfully launch an attack immediately. This kind of attack is typical of Karate and above all, of Jaido and represents a preferred principle.

Go no Sen

This principle contains a counterattack in a defensive situation (position). With regard to the opponent's attack this means that you can weave and dodge his attack, apply a soft defensive technique and attack him hard immediately. This is a very effective tactical action, if the opponent attacks hard and powerfully. In this case, a trial of strength is unwise from a tactical point of view. The soft principle has decisive advantages. If you apply So no Sen, you must move forward on an imaginary line, if you apply Go no Sen, you must move backwards and then forwards in a classical way (swinging in and out)

Tai Sabaki

Tai Sabaki means that you escape from an attack by turning away and that you thus get yourself into a good position for an attack. This is a typical tactical basic principle which is often made use of in Aikido. At the same time it means that you keep your balance in order to cause your opponent to fall and to overpower him. By changing the angle of the attack you can reduce the power of your opponent's attack and can get into a superior starting position. Logically, the direction of the movement is always sideways. Usually, these movements provide an ideal opportunity to prepare a throw as it is usual in Judo. With a weapon, such movements are quick and effective, especially if you use a long stick.

Debana o Kujiku

Debana o Kujiku is a surprise attack. It means that you overpower your opponent by a surprise attack with the help of a diversionary maneuver. Here the effect depends on the precise chronological initiative by starting the surprise attack. This is often very difficult, but it represents an important technique in Jaido. The different tactical principles, which have been described, represent the essential part of possible techniques. However, there are a great number of further variations.

A clever tactician can be compared with a shuairan. The shuairan is a snake which lives in the Chang Mountains. Hit its head and its tail will attack you; hit its tail and its head will attack you; hit its centre and its head and tail will attack you.

Sunzi

7 INSTRUCTION IN BO-JUTSU

Bo-Jutsu is a Kobudo discipline which is closely connected to other Japanese martial arts (such as Karate, Jujutsu, Aikido, and others) because of its patterns of movement. Originally, it was the norm that training in martial arts comprised training in techniques with and without weapons. Among them were Kenjutsu (sword fighting), Kyujutsu (archery), Sojutsu (throwing the spear) and Kumi uchi (fighting without weapons – Yawara).

More modern disciplines such as Aikido, Judo, Jujutsu and partly Karate were developed from Kumi Uchi. The special influences from different countries such as China or Korea, which arrived via the Okinawa Islands, shall not be dealt with in detail. It is so obvious that the system of movements and the systematic approaches of the various disciplines are strongly related to each other. The possibilities of attack on a human body cannot change and the wheel need not be invented anew.

That is why it is a good idea to have gained valuable and extensive experience in another martial art, another system of movement and other basic principles before you start Bo-Jutsu. I explicitly warn teachers not to pass their knowledge of weapon arts on to children or immature adolescents; you have to individually decide each case on its own merits, because dealing with weapons requires much circumspection and perfect discipline in order to avoid damage and injuries to another person.

The principles of the modern concept of Budo must be absolutely obligatory. Among them are: the greatest respect for the fellow pupil and the teacher, the limitation of the martial art to the dojo or similar institutions; hard and permanent training and devotion to the traditional values are decisive. The best way for Budo to have an effect on day-to-day life is to respect and observe social values, to hold individuals in high esteem, to develop powers of self-assertion and self-confidence.

Motokatsu Inoue put into words some basic phrases, which are mentioned here:
1. Dodge the opponent not by power, but by your body, and place yourself in the best position.
2. Continue to practice constantly all through your life.
3. Karate and Ryukyu martial arts are quite the same originally.

4. Study the spirit which comprises Rei, Zanshin and so on, in the process of studying Bujutsu.

5. You must be able to use weapons, but never depend on them.

In the wider sense, as many things in Budo, this advice can be transferred to everyday life and help to solve problems correctly while taking social values into consideration.

The student goes through different stages of development, faster or not so fast, depending on his previous knowledge or talent.

STAGE 1

Stage 1 consists of getting acquainted with the Bo. The movements are often strange and clumsy. The normal flexibility of the body seems to be paralyzed. It is a typical beginner's mistake that they make no effort to use the whole body, which is essential for Asian martial arts. That is why the beginner's techniques for using the Bo are ineffective. The handling of the Bo must become second nature to the beginner without him having to look at the Bo. For this reason at the beginning of Stage 1, simple and circular movements must be trained and repeated again and again.

Again and again the teacher must remind the student to practice without power but with kinetic energy. In this way natural movements develop without an increased risk of injury. It is vitally important that the student understands that most of the movements of the Bo consist of sectors of circles or ellipses.

STAGE 2

Stage 2 is characterized by the fact that the student has a good command of simple techniques (such as Uke-defense, Tsuki-poke, Uchi-blow) at least from a standing position. Now the teacher has to keep an eye on the student's position, the acceleration of the weapon and the way of locking it. In addition, there are simple combinations of steps, e.g. stepping on the spot, simply gliding forward and backward, a sideways movement. Again and again the teacher must show his student how to make use of every body movement to accelerate the Bo effectively. The student's efforts will finally meet with some success. No movement must be superfluous. The relation of these techniques to the techniques of Karate and to the basic principles of Iaido (acceleration, change of position while making most of centrifugal forces, **Mai** = feeling of distance) must be explained again and again. Students tend to internalize this very slowly and it often takes many years. It is vitally important that the student understands that in real life it all depends whether he can make use of simple techniques in a tactically clever way (cf. the chapter on tactics).

Not all the techniques and combinations which are practiced are suitable for use in real life, e.g. in Kumibo. They must be practiced anyway. The same applies to Karate and other disciplines. The exercises serve their purpose of training the coordination, take-off power, balance, strength, hardening, stretching and flexibility of the whole body. Furthermore, the senses, especially the instinct to behave and to act in a particular way, and the sense of sight, must be trained so that in real life the techniques and the use of simple combinations function automatically, even faster and better without thinking about them.

Stage 3

Stage 3 leads to expertise. At this stage, difficult combinations are called for, which have to contribute to the feelings of coordination, mobility and flexibility up at maximum effect. In the course of this stage, many tasks have to be coped with and carried out in order to put the final touches to the Budoka. They lead to the ultimate refinement of the higher Master grades, which deal with an understanding of the human body, basic medical knowledge of the human anatomy, reflexive zones, vital points **(Kyusho)** and Kuatsu (the Japanese technique of resuscitation). The final stage is not a topic of this book, because it is the Master who teaches his student directly and personally. It is a question of mutual confidence.

There are some issues at this stage I want to deal with: among other things, how to improve one's **balance** and how to develop a better feeling of one's **center of gravity**. Both are the prerequisites for strong and quick techniques. A standing position, which is too low, gives stability and a firm hold with your feet, but speed, mobility and flexibility lessen.

The other way round, a high standing position and a high center of gravity lack stability and the release of energy is reduced. Every student must learn this individually. Furthermore, the concentration of power **(Kime)** must be improved. This is impossible without correct breathing. Maximum inhalation is looked upon as weakness, maximum exhalation as strength. That means poke, blow and defense must be carried out at the point of optimal exhalation.

Everybody who has practiced any kind of martial art knows this feeling of strength **(Kime)**. As I already mentioned above, every technique is ineffective without correct acceleration. Even the beginner can re-enact this with a long weapon. That is why I strongly recommend that every Karateka should practice with a stick (Jo, Hanbo, or Bo). His techniques without weapons will improve as well. Whoever always practices with permanent tension will soon tire, will be too slow and will not be able to strike an effective blow.

You must accelerate as lithely as a tiger and you must be as hard as rock for a short moment when you hit your opponent (Kime). That is the road to success. Whoever moves monotonously in an unchanging constant **rhythm** will never strike an effective blow. Correct rhythm is both slow and fast and thus it is difficult to foresee what you are planning. Short moments of tension alternate with moments of relaxation. Both martial arts and folk dances live on rhythm.

This can also be transferred to everyday life. Myamoto Musashi, one of the most famous Japanese sword fighters, said: "The most important thing is the correct point of time and the correct rhythm." Musashi mentions the second decisive aspect: namely time or **timing** as it is called in martial arts. Without correct timing there are no hits in offensive or defensive actions. The different tactical possibilities (Sen no Sen, Go no Sen and Tai Sabaki) have already been dealt with.

Running parallel to these stages of development, the practice of Katas (forms) with different levels of difficulty, training with a partner (Bunkei, Kihon Kumibo, Jiyu Ippon Kumibo, Happo Kumibo and Jiu Kumibo) and instruction on self-defense must take place.

World seminar of the IMAF Kokusai Budoin, Düsseldorf Germany 2003.

In the center from the left to the right:
A.Frederix 8[th]Dan Aikido Kyoshi, Prof.Sato 10[th]Dan Nihon Jujutsu Hanshi,
9[th]Dan Judo Hanshi, HD Rauscher 8[th]Dan Karate Hanshi, 6[th]Dan Kobudo Kyoshi,
7[th]Dan Iaido Kyoshi a.o., K.Tose 10[th]Dan Iaido Hanshi, S.Higushi 9[th]Dan Karate
Hanshi, 7[th]Dan Kobudo Kyoshi, M.Kondo 9[th]Dan Judo Hanshi, 7[th]Dan Aikido Kyoshi,
6[th]Dan Karate Kyoshi

Training for Children in the Dojo of Master Tetsuhiro Hokama (Nishihara Okinawa March 2004)

Goju Ryu Training in the Dojo of Sensei T. Hokama in Okinawa

8   WARMING-UP AND GYMNASTICS

The warming-up exercise takes place from top to bottom (head, neck, arms, spinal cord, hips, legs) in connection with a massage with the stick. After this, stretching exercises with the stick follow and in addition, different exercises to strengthen the wrists can be done.

Regular and light exercise at the beginning which gradually becomes more vigorous is safer and more effective and helps to avoid injuries (tenosynovitis caused by overexertion). You cannot ignore the fact that general physical fitness and abilities differ a lot. If physical weaknesses cannot be corrected, modified techniques and stamina training must be used to compensate (e.g. weak wrists, a blocked hip, and others).

Some schools do not do gymnastics. They are of the opinion that there is no warming-up phase in a real fight. If you want to enjoy lifelong good health, I think you should better start your training after the salutation with warming-up, stretching and strengthening exercises. At the beginning, you will start at a low level, which will be increased in the course of advanced training. In the following, a selection of typical examples is presented.

A bamboo cane does not fear the storm, because it is flexible.
Japanese wise saying

WARMING-UP AND GYMNASTICS

Bending the upper part of the body

Bending to the side

Hip rotation

Vertical movement with hip rotation

Stretching one's shoulders

Sliding one's hands on the left, Keashi Mochikae

Sliding one's hands in front

Sliding one's hands on the right

Rotating the Bo between one's fingers

Massaging one's shoulder by tapping

Steeling one's arms and wrists by moving the Bo forwards and backwards

Steeling one's arms and wrists by rotating

9 BASIC TECHNIQUES

Holding the Bo (Mochi, Nigiri)
Stances (Dachi)
Etiquette, Bow (Re)
Keeping ready (Yoi)
Starting to fight (Hajime)
Finishing (Naore)
Targets

Holding the Bo

There are many differences between several Kobudo schools regarding Gyaku Mochi; that means changing the grip out of the Honte Mochi position. Gyaku Nigiri is called Heiko Mochi in Matayoshi Kobudo.

Beginners have to hold the Bo with the distance between the hands corresponding to the width of the shoulders. In an upper level of training the distance between the hands varies in different situations. The movements of the hands depend on the distance to the target.

Honte Mochi = Jun Nigiri

Gyakute Mochi = Gyaku Nigiri

*In **Nagate Mochi** the distance between the hands corresponds to the width of the shoulders (Effects: larger radius, greater impact)*

Yose Mochi = Yose Nigiri

Hasami Mochi = Hasami Nigiri

Mochikake (Changing the Grip)

Direct Change (without moving the Bo) **Jun Mochikake**

Changing the grip by sliding (180° Move of the Bo)   **Kaeshi Mochikake**

ATTENTION: Hold the Bo tight, do not throw it!

During a fight, holding (Jun Mochikake) the Bo tight is much safer than sliding it (Kaeshi Mochikake). So the Bo cannot easily be pushed out of your hands. Kaeshi Mochikake is faster and more elegant, but in a fight the Bo can be hit out of your grip and you might run the risk of losing it.

STANCES (DACHI)

Heiko Dachi
(Natural Stance I)
Feet parallel, distance corresponding
to the width of the shoulders

Soto Hachiji Dachi
(Natural Stance II)
Distance as described above,
feet pointing outwards

Heisoku Dachi
(Ready Stance I)

Musubi Dachi
(Ready Stance II)

Zenkutsu Dachi (Forward Stance)

Gyaku (or Okinawa) Zenkutsu Dachi (Rear Defensive Stance)

Kokutsu Dachi (Back Stance)

Nekoashi Dachi (Cat Stance)

Sanchin Dachi (Inner Tension Stance)

Sochin (Fudo) Dachi (Outer Tension Stance)

Kiba (Naifanchi) **Dachi** (Horse Stance)

Shiko Dachi (Straddle Stance)

Uchi Hachiji Dachi
(Inversed Open Stance)

Rei No Ji Dachi (V-Stance)

Sagi Ashi Dachi (Shirasagiashi Dachi) (Crane Stance)

Kousa Dachi (Cross Stance)

ETIQUETTE, RE (BOW)

RE   FRONT VIEW   Side View

Yoi (PREPARE)
Yoi   FRONT VIEW   Side View

Hajime (Starting Position)
Hajime (Ready stance, feet on the same line)

Front View

Side View

Hajime (Ready stance, left foot in front)

Front View

Side View

Naore
(Finishing)

At the end (Naore) the Bo has to be held in the middle of the body in order to maintain preparedness to fight (Zanshin).

Both your hands hold the Bo until you are sure that the opponent will not start any further attack. Thereafter your left hand will be moved to your left upper thigh. Finally the Bo has to be moved to the right hand side.

Front View   **Side View**

TARGETS (Selection of Vital Points – Kyusho)

Coronary Suture **Tento, Tendo**	Temple (Yoko Men) **Kasumi**	Side of Neck **Matzukaz**

Throat **Nodo Botoke**	Solar Plexus **Mizo ochi/Suigettsu**	Groin/Upper Thigh/Testis **Yako/Kintek**

Elbow **Hijitsume**	Wrist (Kote) **Shuko**	Knee **Shitsu to**

Foot   **Kori/-Sokko**

The Back of the Neck   **Keichu**

Spine   **Kassatsu**

The Back of the Knee   **Hiza Kubomi**

B SPECIAL PART

BASICS (Kihon) I

The basic techniques are restricted to a few exercises, which are essential at the beginning of the study of Kobujutsu. To these belong: the fighting positions (Kamae), the defensive techniques (Uke) and the offensive techniques (Seme). In the following, some techniques are compiled, which can be successfully practiced with a partner (cf. basic exercises). If they both have theses techniques under control, defensive techniques can be combined with offensive techniques in such a way that they can be practiced with a partner without problems. The techniques can also be practiced in forms of Katas and that is why they are easy to learn. The patterns taken from simple Katas can be used for the practice of basic techniques (e.g. from Taikyoku Shodan – chudan, jodan, gedan, and so on). These Katas help to make practice without a group or a partner easier.

The Kamae Kata, Uke Kata and Seme Kata are practiced according to the conventional rules of etiquette, that means: you start with the formal salutation (Re), followed by the standby position (Yoi), the start position (Hajime); you finish with the dissolution (Naore) and the formal salutation at the end.

Whoever has the technique under control is not yet master.
Piece of Zen wisdom

1   BASICS (Kihon I)

Etiquette (Bow)

Fighting Position (Kamae)

Kamae Kata

Block Techniques (Uke Waza)

Uke Kata

Attacks (Seme Waza)

Seme Kata

Etiquette (Bow)

Re   **Front View**   **Side View**

READY Position (Yoi)   STARTING (Hajime)

Left arm above the eyes in order to achieve a clear view

NAORE (Finishing)   RE (Bow)

Kamae Kata (Fighting Positions/Forms)

Re, Yoi, Hajime

Front View   **Side View**

1. Chudan Kamae

2. Gedan Kamae

FRONT VIEW   **Side View**

3. Jodan Kamae

4. Waki Kamae

5. Hasso Kamae

NAORE, RE

Uke Kata (Defensive Kata)

Re, Yoi, Hajime

Front View **Side View**

1. Soto Uke

2. Uchi Uke

FRONT VIEW

SIDE VIEW

3. Sukui Uke (back)

4. Gedan (Osae) Uke (back)

5. Harai Uke (ahead)

NAORE, RE

Seme Kata (Attacks/Forms)

Re, Yoi, Hajime

Front View   **Side View**

1. Nuki Tsuki

2. Maede Tsuki

FRONT VIEW   ## SIDE VIEW

3. Gedan Nuki Tsuki

4. Jodan Uchi

5. Furiage Uchi

6. Yoko Uchi

7. Ura Uchi

Naore, Re

BASICS (Kihon) II

Advanced techniques belong to Basics (Kihon) II which must be practiced both on the left and on the right. They must be carried out in an equilateral and reciprocal (Gyaku) position. Furthermore, advanced defensive and offensive techniques belong to this. In addition, simple combinations are practiced, which represent the beginning of a smooth motion with several techniques. It seems to be essential that the combinations are not only carried out in one direction (forward and backward) but in different directions and that they are repeated again and again. The practice can also be successfully performed in patterns from simple Katas. Some typical separate techniques and some examples of exercises of combinations are presented in the following.

> *"In every war our main objective shall be a decisive victory
> and not a lengthy campaign."*
>
> Sunzi – The Art of War

2. BASICS (Kihon) II

Block Techniques (Uke Waza)
Jodan (upper level)
Chudan (middle level)
Gedan (lower level)
Special Forms (Hikake, Mamori, Sunakake)

Attacks (Seme Waza)
Thrust (Tsuki)
Strikes (Uchi)

Combinations

Kihon II
Uke Waza   Block Techniques

Morote Uke (Jodan, Chudan, Gedan, Ushiro)

Jodan   Age Uke
               Sukui Uke

Chudan   Soto Uke
               Uchi Uke
               Tate Uke

Gedan   Harai Uke
               Gedan Uke
               Osae Uke

Special Forms Hikake
               Mamori
               Sunakake

Morote Uke

Double Block

Jodan Morote Uke on the right

Jodan Morote Uke on the left

Chudan Morote Uke

Gyaku Chudan Morote Uke

Gedan Morote Uke on the right

Gedan Morote Uke on the left

Ushiro Morote Uke

Gyaku Ushiro Morote Uke

Jodan Uke

Blocks Upper Level

Age Uke

Gyaku Age Uke

Sukui Uke on the right

Sukui Uke on the left

Chudan Uke

Blocks Middle Level

Soto (Yoko) Uke Block from inside to outside

Gyaku Soto Uke

Uchi (Yoko) Uke Block from outside to inside

Gyaku Uchi Uke

Tate (Mae) Uke   Vertical Block

Gyaku Tate Uke

Gedan Uke

Blocks Lower Level

Harai Uke

Gyaku Harai Uke

Gedan Uke

Gyaku Gedan Uke

(Gedan) Osae Uke on the left

Osae Uke on the right

SPECIAL FORMS

Hikake Round Block

Gyaku Hikake

Mamori Defensive Posture

Gyaku Mamori

Sunakake   Block from the lower to
the inner and upper level

Kihon II

Seme Waza   Attacks

Tsuki   **Thrust**

Morote (Maede) Tsuki
Nuki Tsuki
Nagashi Tsuki
Furi Tsuki

Uchi   **Strikes**

Jodan   Jodan Uchi
                   Naname Uchi
                   Kesa Uchi
                   Age Uchi
                   Morote Uchi
                   Yoko Men Uchi

Chudan   Yoko Uchi
                   Ura Uchi

Gedan   Gedan Uchi
                   Gedan Uchi Barai

Tsuki   **THRUST**

Chudan Morote Tsuki (double handed thrust)

Gyaku Morote Tsuki

Jodan Morote Tsuki

Gyaku Jodan Morote Tsuki

Gedan Morote Tsuki

Gyaku Gedan Morote Tsuki

Chudan Nuki Tsuki (sliding thrust)   Gyaku Chudan Nuki Tsuki

Jodan Nuki Tsuki   Gyaku Jodan Nuki Tsuki

Otoshi Tsuki   Gyaku Otoshi Tsuki

Jodan Nagashi Tsuki

Gyaku Jodan Nagashi Tsuki

Furi Tsuki 1

Furi Tsuki 2

Furi Tsuki 3

The difference between Morote (Maede) Tsuki and Nuki Tsuki:
Morote Tsuki is a double handed thrust; both hands remain tightly on the staff. Nuki Tsuki is a sliding thrust. Only the back hand remains tightly on the staff. The hand in front fixes the target; the staff slides through the hand in front.

Uchi   STRIKES

Jodan (Otoshi) Shomen Uchi (strike to the top of the head)   Gyaku Shomen Uchi

Naname Uchi (strike to the temple)   Gyaku Naname Uchi

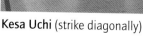 

Kesa Uchi (strike diagonally)   Gyaku Kesa Uchi

Age Uchi (upper strike)

Gyaku Age Uchi

Jodan Morote Uchi (double upper strike)

Gedan Morote Uchi

Yoko Men (Jodan) Uchi (strike to the side of the head)

Gyaku Yoko Men Uchi

Chudan Yoko Uchi (strike to the side of the body)   **Gyaku Chudan Yoko Uchi**

Chudan Ura Uchi (reverse strike to the body)   **Gedan Ura Uchi**

Gedan Uchi (strike downwards)   **Gyaku Gedan Uchi**

Gedan Uchi Barai (strike diagonally down)

Kihon II (Advanced Basics)

Combination 1
Waki Kamae, Kesa Uchi, Osae Uke, Gedan Nuki Tsuki

Combination 2
Waki Kamae, Yoko Uchi, Ura Uchi

Combination 3
Waki Kamae, Kesa Uchi, Age, Otoshi Uchi

Combination 4
Chudan Kamae, Osae Uke, Gedan Uke, Shomen Uchi

Combination 5
Chudan Kamae, Soto Uke, Ura Morote Uchi

Combination 6
Waki Kamae, Yoko Uchi, Yoko Uchi

Combination 7
Chudan Kamae, Naname Uchi, Furi Tsuki

Combination 8
Waki Kamae, Jodan Uchi, Nuki Tsuki

Combination 9
Chudan Kamae, Yoko Men Uchi, Ura Uchi

Combination 10
Chudan Kamae, Age Uchi, Otoshi Uchi

COMBINATIONS

COMBINATION 1

Waki Kamae

Kesa Uchi/Shiko Dachi/Prepare

Osae Uke   OZ

Gedan Nuki Tsuki   OZ

*(for abbreviations
see Page 129)*

COMBINATION 2

Waki Kamae   ZD

Yoko Uchi   SD

Ura Uchi   ZK

Yoko Uchi   SD

Combination 3

Waki Kamae ZD   *Kesa Uchi SD*   *Age Uchi ZD*   *Otoshi Uchi ZD*

Combination 4

Chudan Kamae ZD   *Osae Uke OZ*   *Gedan Uke SD*   *Shomen Uchi ZD*

Combination 5

Chudan Kamae ZD   *Soto Uke ZD*   *Prepare*   *Ura Morote Uchi ZD*

Combination 6

Waki Kamae   ZD

Yoko Uchi   SD

Changing hands

Yoko Uchi   ZD

Combination 7

Chudan Kamae   ZD

Naname Uchi   ZD

Prepare

Furi Tsuki ZD

Combination 8

Waki Kamae   ZD

Prepare

Jodan Uchi   ZD

Nuki Tsuki ZD

Prepare

Jodan Uchi   ZD

Nuki Tsuki   ZK

Prepare and so on

Combination 9

Chudan Kamae   ZD

Yoko Men Uchi   ZD

Ura Uchi   ZK

Prepare

Yoko Men Uchi   ZD

Ura Uchi   ZD

Combination 10

Chudan Kamae   ZD

Age Uchi   ZD

Otoshi Uchi   ZD

Prepare

Jodan Uchi   ZD

Age Uchi   ZD

Otoshi Uchi and so on

BASICS (KiHON) III

The essential subject matter of the advanced elementary school consists of the complex movements of different combinations. These complex movements require a lot of practice, which must be based upon the Basic Techniques I and II. It is important for the pupils to have these techniques under control both clockwise and anticlockwise.

It is necessary for them to practice and repeat these movements in any direction in order to learn how to perform realistic offensive and defensive movements more and more perfectly.

In the following, some examples of exercises are presented which belong to the group of advanced combinations and techniques.

In order to achieve an optimum standard of techniques in regard to leverage, acceleration and keeping the correct distance, it is important for the pupil to repeat constantly, to improve the dynamic force of his body, to make the most of the acceleration of the stick, to use his hips effectively and to keep the center of gravity under control.

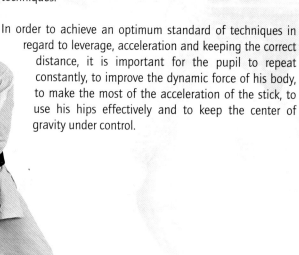

3   BASICS (Kihon) III

Complex Techniques
Ichimonji Mawashi
Mae Mawashi
Hachiji Mawashi
Kata Sukashi
Ushiro Dori
Daisha Mawashi

Combinations

Complex Techniques

Ichimonji Mawashi

Mae Mawashi

Hachiji Mawashi

Kata Sukashi

Ushiro Dori

Daisha Mawashi

Basics (Kihon) III Combinations

Combination 1
Ura Harai Uke, Morote Tsuki, Ura Harai Uke, Gyaku Morote Tsuki

Combination 2
Ichimonji Mawashi, Mae Mawashi

Combination 3
Jodan Kamae, Shomen Uchi, Hachi Mawashi Uchi

Combination 4
Shomen Uchi, Soto Uke

Combination 5
Shomen Uchi, Yoko Uchi, Ura Uchi

Combination 6
Tate Uke, Gedan Uke, Nuki Tsuki, Shomen Uchi

Combination 7
Morote Uke Jodan, Morote Uke Gedan, Morote Uke left, Morote Uke right, Maede Tsuki

Combination 8
Sukuiage Sunakake

Combination 9
Age Uchi, Yoko Men Uchi

Combination 10
Ura Harai Uke, Hachi Mawashi Uchi

All combinations begin with Chudan Kamae:

Combinations

Combination 1

Ura Harai Uke

Morote Tsuki

Ura Harai Uke

Gyaku Morote Tsuki

Combination 2

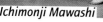

Ichimonji Mawashi

Mae Mawashi

chimonji Mawashi

Mae Mawashi

Combination 3

Jodan Kamae

Shomen Uchi

Hachi Mawashi Uchi

Jodan Kamae

Jodan Uchi

Hachi Mawashi Uchi

Jodan Uchi

Combination 4

Jodan Kamae

Shomen Uchi

Soto Uke

Shomen Uchi

Combination 5

Shomen Uchi

Yoko Uchi

Ura Uchi

Shomen Uchi

Combination 6

Tate Uke

Gedan Uke + Nuki Tsuki

Shomen Uchi

Tate Uke

Combination 7

Iorote Uke Jodan　　*Gedan*　　*Yoko Morote Uke left + right*　　　　*Maede Tsuki*

Combination 8

Sukuiage (catch a staff, turn it to the other side)　　　　*Sunakake*

change of the hands　　*Sukuiage*　　　　*Sunakake*

Combination 9

Age Uchi   *Yoko Men Uchi*   *Age Uchi*   *Yoko Men Uchi*

Combination 10

Ura Harai Uke   *Hachi Mawashi Uchi*

TRAINING WITH A PARTNER

Basic Fighting Techniques

As mentioned above, basic defensive techniques (Uke Kata) can be combined with basic offensive techniques (Seme-Kata). These basic techniques can easily be supplemented with simple separate techniques, as it is presented in the following.

Complicated motions are of no use to typical fighting combinations. In the same way as in Karate, the student's proficiency can be improved if different combinations of offensive and defensive techniques are attached to each other (increase of concentration with help of more extensive and previously agreed series). By analogy with Gohon or Sanbon Kumite (Te stands for hand) in Karate, practicing this with a partner is called Kumibo in Bo-Jutsu (Bo stands for stick).

A further possibility is the defense against several attacks from different opponents, but again you have to watch that these attacks must have been previously agreed on. These forms of exercises are only suitable for advanced students, because lack of concentration and lack of practice risk injury.

There are different stages of fighting with a stick:
1. Yakushu (previously agreed series of combinations),
2. Jiyu Ippon (defence of a single attack previously agreed),
3. Jiju Kumibo (free fight).

Free Fight (Jiju Kumibo)

Nowadays, a string of newly developed safety equipment makes it possible for the student to practice free fight exercises with effectively upholstered long sticks. In spite of the safety equipment blows and stabs at vital parts of the body should be avoided. If you practice such defused free fight, you will soon find out that complicated motions can hardly be used.

By analogy with Kendo, you will be taught that only a few weak points are open to attack and that only a few defensive strategies are possible. The exercises are of vital importance to the development of the reactions and the "eyes".

4 TRAINING WITH A PARTNER

Uke Kata versus Seme Kata
Basic Fighting Training

Ryoanji Tempel in Kyoto

Uke Kata versus Seme Kata (Kumite I)

Attack	Defense
1. Nuki Tsuki	Soto Uke
2. Maede Tsuki	Uchi Uke
3. Gedan Tsuki	Osae Uke
4. Jodan Uchi	Sukui Uke
5. Furi Age Uchi	Morote Uke
6. Gedan Uchi	Harai Uke
7. Yoko Uchi	Hikake
8. Ura Uchi	Mamori

Uke Kata versus Seme Kata

Each Combination begins with Re (bow), Yoi (prepare), Hajime (ready), Kamae (fighting position).

1 Re (Bow)

2

3 Yoi (Prepare)

4

5 Hajime (Ready)

6 Chudan Kamae (Middle Fighting Position)

1. Chudan Kamae

Nuki Tsuki/Soto Uke

2. Chudan Kamae

Maede Tsuki/Uchi Uke

3. Chudan Kamae

Gedan Nuki Tsuki/Osae Uke

4. Jodan Kamae

Jodan Uchi/Sukui Uke

5. Chudan Kamae

Furiage Uchi/Morote Uke

6. Waki Kamae Hasso Kamae

Gedan Uchi/Harai Uke

7. Chudan Kamae
Yoko Uchi/Hikake

8. Chudan Kamae
Ura Uchi/Morote (Yoko) Uke

Each combination ends with Kamae (fighting position) mit Naore (finishing) and Re (bow)

Kamae (Fighting Position)

Naore (Finishing)

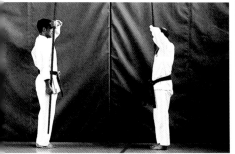

Re (Bow)

Basic Fighting Exercises (Kumite II)

Attack	Defense, Conterattack
1. Jodan Uchi	Naname Uchi, Maede Tsuki
2. Jodan Uchi	Sukui Uke, Ura Uchi
3. Jodan Uchi	Morote Uke, Juji Jime, Ashi Barai, Shomen Uchi
4. Chudan Maede Tsuki	Uchi Uke, Yoko Men Uchi
5. Chudan Maede Tsuki	Soto Uke, Shomen Uchi
6. Chudan Yoko Uchi	Morote Uke, Age Uchi, Otoshi Uchi
7. Chudan Ura Uchi	Morote Uke, Shomen Uchi
8. Gedan Uchi	Harai Uke, Sukuiage, Sunakake, Jodan Uchi
9. Gedan Uchi	Osae Uke, Gedan Uchi, Shomen Uchi
10. Gedan Uchi	Mamori, Gedan Uchi, Shomen Uchi

Basic-Fighting Combinations (Kihon Kumite II)

Beginning with:

1. Re (Bow)

2.

3. Yoi (Prepare)

4. Hajime (Ready)

5. z. B. Chudan Kamae (Middle Fighting Position)

As in all the combinations with a partner, each of the exercises begin with the bow (Re), the prepare (Yoi), the ready to fight (Hajime) and the actual fighting stance (Kamae). They end with the finish (Naore) and the bow (Re). Breaks in training are particularly necessary for beginners to balance the training exercises and to permit the partners to concentrate better. In this way, injuries caused by uncontrolled techniques can safely be avoided.

Attack Upper Level (Jodan)

1. Chudan Kamae

Jodan Uchi/Naname Uchi

Morote Tsuki

2. Chudan Kamae

Jodan Uchi/Sukui Uke

Gedan Ura Uchi

3. Chudan Kamae

Jodan Uchi/Morote Uke   Juji Jime + Ashi Barai (Choking + forward foot sweep) Shomen Uchi

Attack to Middle Level (Chudan)

| 4. Chudan Kamae | Chudan Morote Tsuki/Uchi Uke | Yoko Men Uchi |

| 5. Chudan Kamae | Chudan Maede Tsuki/Soto Uke | Shomen Uchi |

6. Chudan Kamae
Chudan Yoko Uchi/
      Morote Uke   Age Uchi   Otoshi Uchi

7. Chudan Kamae   Ura Uchi/Morote Uke   Shomen Uchi

Attack to Lower Level (Gedan)

8. Chudan Kamae
Gedan Uchi/Harai Uke   /Sukuiage Sunakake   /Jodan Uchi

9. Chudan Kamae
Gedan Nuki Tsuki/Osae Uke   /Gedan Uchi   /Shomen Uchi

10. Gedan Uchi/ Mamori   /Gedan Uchi   /Shomen Uchi

Ending with:

1. NAORE (Finishing)

2. RE (Bow)

5   FORMS (KATAS)

A lot of Katas have been developed for the long stick. Chinese origins are more or less noticeable. Some famous Masters have developed traditional Chinese Katas further or they have invented new ones. As the Katas were mainly passed down through verbal instruction and the old face-to-face teaching methods from instructors to students, there are hardly any available written sources. That is why a lot of Katas have been lost. The closure of dojos and the events during the invasion of Okinawa at the end of World War II added to this process.

Famous Masters who have developed Katas are Sueshi (Sushi no Kun Sho, Sushi no Kun Dai, Sushi, and others), Sakugawa (Sakugawa no Kun Sho, Sakugawa no Kun Dai, and others) and Shinken Taira, who learnt more than 30 Bo-Katas and put them down in writing. Here again, the analogy with other elements of martial arts is revealing. Different dojos also have different interpretations of Katas. That is why it is not appropriate to say that something is right or wrong if you evaluate the Kata of another dojo. There are for example more than 20 different versions of Sushi no Kun. Master Sueshi had a young servant who watched him secretly when he was practicing Bo. Up to that time Sueshi had no close student. One day he noticed his curious onlooker and confronted him about it. He noticed that his servant was seriously interested in Kobudo. After some time he realized that he was talented and he put his trust in him. Later this student developed the Kata further, improved it and developed three more forms.

Some variants of this Kata, and also of the Sushi no Kun Dai Kata are presented in the following. In parts, the differences are insignificant. It is vitally important that you know one form (Kata), which enables you to practice the techniques learned before. Doubtlessly, it will be to your advantage, if you are acquainted with different dojos.

In order to elucidate the historical perspective with reference to Ufugusuku no Kun and Oshiro no Kun, I want to add an explanatory note which was provided by Sensei Tetsuhiro Hokama during my study trip to Okinawa in the town of Nishihara. His grandfather, who gave him his first lessons in Karate, was a direct neighbor of Mr Ufugusuku, a Master of Kobudo and an expert in long sticks. He lived very close to Shuri-jo Castle. That is why Sensei Tetsuhiro Hokama has preserved the probably most authentic form of the Kata, which I present in this book as "Hokama Version".

Master Ufugusuku's second first name was Oshiro. So that is what it is all about. The Katas of the Shorin Ryu school of Master Shinzato contain both Ufugusuku No

Kun and Kata Oshiro No Kun. Both Katas differ from the probably original Kata in so far that they have been essentially simplified and it is only when certain techniques are combined that the original Kata becomes recognizable. The simplification of original Katas and of Bo respective Karate techniques can be found everywhere. The realistic use (application) was often neglected or forgotten. The activation of acupressure on particular points of the body in order to improve one's health and strength has often been neglected in the same way as attacks at vital points of the opponent (Kyusho). Thus Katas are partly falsified to such an extent that they no longer work.

It is important for the pupils to keep in mind that Katas are forms of practice with a real background and that they must not be mistaken for ballet. While practicing a Kata, the students must imagine the real actions of a fight. Furthermore, the use (application) of the Kata must be clear and effective (Bunkai).

The following characteristics are of great importance during a presentation of a Kata: Zanshin (readiness to fight), Kime (use of strength/energy), correct breathing, rhythm and exact techniques.

Patrick McCarthy has summarized the essential principles of Katas in his book "Ancient Okinawan Martial Arts":

Yoi no kishin	mental preparation
Inyo	comprehension of cause and effect
Go no sen, sen no sen and sen	principles of initiative
Mai	a sense of the correct distance (mai) and tai sabaki
Tai no shinshuku	tension and relaxation (muscle, movement)
Chikara no kyojaku	correct use of strength/energy with every technique
Kiai-jutsu	correct use of the flow of strength (Ki)
Waza no kankyu	speed and rhythm of the technique
Ju no ri	principle of reassurance and holding out against a hail of attacks
Kokyu	synchronization of breathing depends on tension and relaxation
Bunkai	comprehension of the application/use
Zanshin	permanent readiness to fight (attention)
Seishi o choetzu	suppression of any thoughts to life and death

The patterns of the traditional Katas which are presented in the following are just one possible interpretation of the motions and do not claim to be binding general directions.

The first version of Sushi no Kun Sho represents a simple form which is practiced in many dojos. The second version closely follows the IMAF Kokusai Budoin (I. Higushi, S. Sakai, H. D. Rauscher). The third version is a modification according to F. Demura. Finally, the fourth version is a modification according to Tetsuhiro Hokama.

The different variants of this Kata illustrate the differences and the elements which they have in common. They all seem to stem from an archetype and it seems reasonable to assume that this archetype might be found in Suji No Kun (Yamani Ryu) or in Sushi No Kun (Matayoshi Kobudo). The different versions of Sushi No Kun Dai also provide evidence that they have the same origin as Sushi No Kun or Sushi No Kun Sho.

Again, the first version of Sushi No Kun Dai is an interpretation of the IMAF, and the second version is an interpretation of Tetsuhiro Hokama. The analysis of the Katas Ufugusuku no Kun and Oshiro no Kun from Shorin Ryu is very interesting, especially in comparison with the version Ufugusuku no Kun of Master Hokama.

A real Master does not teach students, he forms new Masters.
Robert Schumann

Tetsuhiro Hokama Ph. D.,
9th Dan Karate/ Kobudo
Hanshi

BO-JUTSU KATAS

Kihon Katas *
1. Kamae Kata
2. Uke Kata
3. Seme Kata

Traditional Katas
Yamani Ryu
1. Sujii no Kun *
2. Choun no Kun Sho **
3. Choun no Kun Dai **
4. Ryubi no Kun **
Ryu Kyu Kobudo (Shorin Ryu)
1. Ufugusuku no Kun *
2. Oshiro no Kun **
Different other Schools
1. Sushi no Kun Sho (Version 1) **
2. Sushi no Kun Sho (Version 2) **
3. Sushi no Kun Sho (Version 3) **
4. Sushi no Kun Sho (Version 4) **
5. Sushi no Kun Dai (Version 1) ***
6. Sushi no Kun Dai (Version 2) ***
7. Sakugawa no Kon (Version 1)***
Okinawan and international Kenshikai Karate Kobudo Association
1. Ufugusuku no Kun (probably original version) ***
Bunkai ***
2. Kumi Bo Ichi (Exercise Kata) **
Bunkai ***

Level of difficulty:
*The Katas have markers * according to the level:*
*   means simple
* *   is advanced
* * * means very difficult

Legend of the Kata Sequences

The sequences of traditional Katas have to be read from left to right. In most cases correspondent techniques are arranged in a vertical row. That is the reason why side view projections are not nessessary in most cases.

Kihon Katas have to be read from top to bottom (Kamae Kata, Uke Kata, Seme Kata).

In order to prevent an overload in the sequences the etiquette is not demonstrated in each graphics (Re, Yoi, Hajime, Naore, Re). If you demonstrate one of these Katas, you have to show this etiquette (look for example in Sujii no Kun).

In the graphics you find the name of the technique in the first row of the text, in the second row you find the stances.

The Kiai (shout with a maximum of Kime) is practiced in different positions of the Kata depending the school and style. In most cases, Kiai is found during the final technique. Because of theses differences, the Kiai is not marked in every sequence.

Abbreviations

Z/Zk	Zenkutsu Dachi
S/SD	Shiko Dachi
OZ/OZk	Okinawa Zenkutsu Dachi
Kk	Kokutsu Dachi
ND	Nekoashi Dachi
HS	Heisuku Dachi oder Heiko Dachi
M = MS = MD	Musubi Dachi
RNJ	Rei no Ji Dachi
Sag	Sagiashi Dachi
Ks	Kousa Dachi

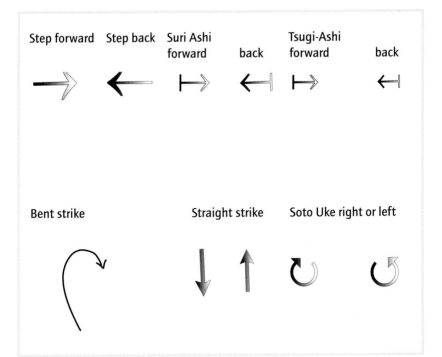

KAMAE KATA

Re

Yoi

Hajime

Front view

Chudan Kamae

Side view

Gedan Kamae

Jodan Kamae

Waki Kamae

Hasso Kamae

Naore

Re

UKE KATA

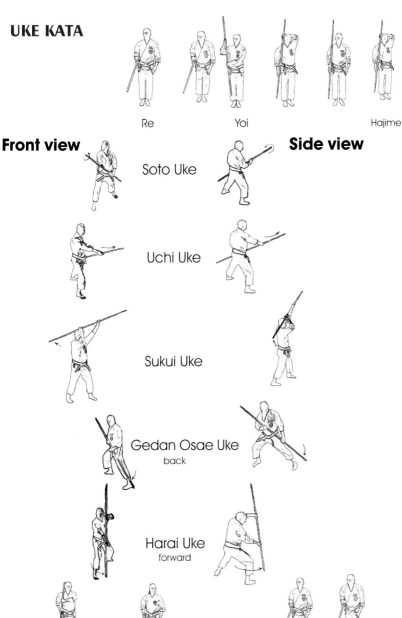

Re   Yoi   Hajime

Front view   **Side view**

Soto Uke

Uchi Uke

Sukui Uke

Gedan Osae Uke
back

Harai Uke
forward

Naore   Re

SEME KATA

Re Yoi Hajime

Front view **Side view**

Nuki Tsuki

Maede Tsuki

Gedan Nukite

Jodan Uchi

Furiage Uchi

Yoko Uchi

Ura Uchi

Naore Re

SUJII NO KUN

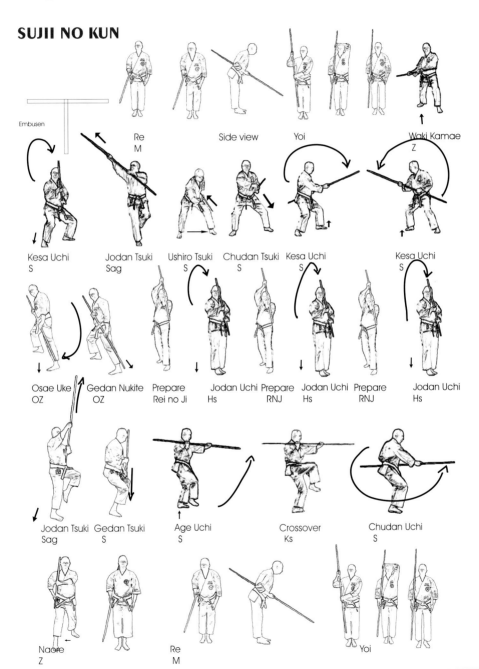

Embusen

Re
M

Side view

Yoi

Waki Kamae
Z

Kesa Uchi
S

Jodan Tsuki
Sag

Ushiro Tsuki
S

Chudan Tsuki
S

Kesa Uchi
S

Kesa Uchi
S

Osae Uke
OZ

Gedan Nukite
OZ

Prepare
Rei no Ji

Jodan Uchi
Hs

Prepare
RNJ

Jodan Uchi
Hs

Prepare
RNJ

Jodan Uchi
Hs

Jodan Tsuki
Sag

Gedan Tsuki
S

Age Uchi
S

Crossover
Ks

Chudan Uchi
S

Naore
Z

Re
M

Yoi

CHOUN NO KUN SHO

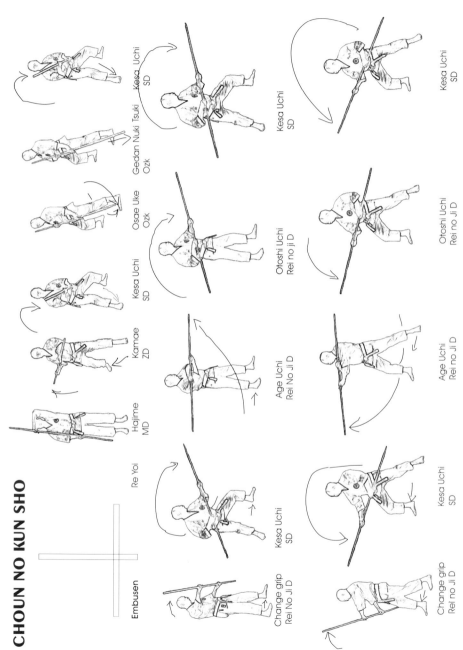

Kesa Uchi
SD

Gedan Nuki Tsuki
Ozk

Osae Uke
Ozk

Kesa Uchi
SD

Kamae
ZD

Hajime
MD

Re Yoi

Embusen

Kesa Uchi
SD

Otoshi Uchi
Rei no Ji D

Age Uchi
Rei No Ji D

Kesa Uchi
SD

Change grip
Rei No Ji D

Kesa Uchi
SD

Otoshi Uchi
Rei no Ji D

Age Uchi
Rei no Ji D

Kesa Uchi
SD

Change grip
Rei no Ji D

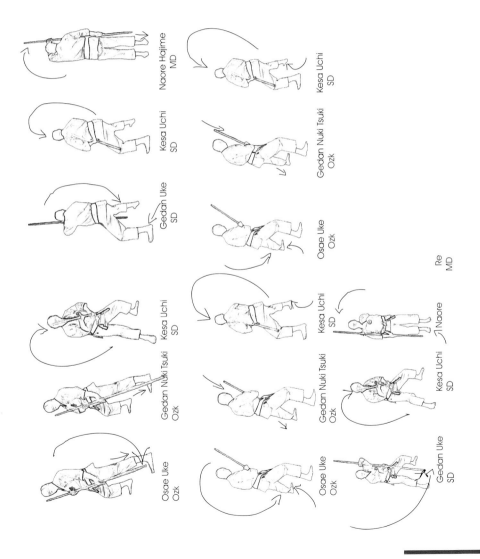

CHOUN NO KUN DAI

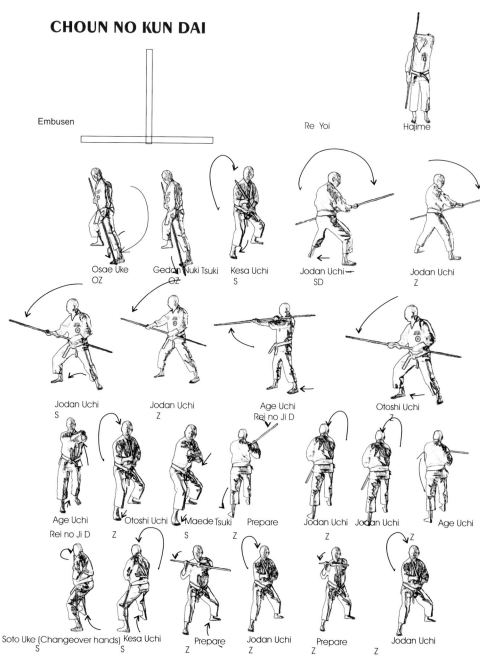

Embusen

Re Yoi

Hajime

Osae Uke
OZ

Gedan Nuki Tsuki
OZ

Kesa Uchi
S

Jodan Uchi
SD

Jodan Uchi
Z

Jodan Uchi
S

Jodan Uchi
Z

Age Uchi
Rei no Ji D

Otoshi Uchi
Z

Age Uchi
Rei no Ji D

Otoshi Uchi
Z

Maede Tsuki
S

Prepare
Z

Jodan Uchi
Z

Jodan Uchi

Age Uchi
Z

Soto Uke (Changeover hands)
S

Kesa Uchi
S

Prepare
Z

Jodan Uchi
Z

Prepare
Z

Jodan Uchi

Waki Kamae
Z

Kesa Uchi
S

Osae Uke
OZ

Gedan Nuki Tsuki
OZ

Kesa Uchi
S

Age Uchi
Rei ni Ji D

Otoshi Uchi

Maede Tsuki
S

Maede Tsuki
S

Jodan Uchi
S

Prepare
Z

Jodan Uchi
Z

Otoshi Uchi
S

Osae Uke
OZ

Kesa Uchi
S

Kesa Uchi (Change grip)
Z

Maede Zuki   Naore   RE
S

RYUBI NO KUN

Embusen

RE Yoi Hajime
Zk

Kesa Uchi
SD

Osae Uke
OZ

Gedan Nuki Tsuki
OZ

Yoi
Heisuku D

Gedan Uke
SD

Jodan Uchi
SD

Age Uchi
Rei no Ji D

Gedan Uke
SD

Jodan Uchi
SD

Age Uchi
Rei no Ji D

Changeover hands
ZK

Prepare
ZK

Osae Uke
OZ

Gedan Nuki Tsuki
OZ

Prepare
Zk

Jodan Kamae
Rei no Ji D

SD

Age Uchi
Rei no Ji D

Kesa Uchi
SD

Jodan Kamae

Jodan Uchi
Zk

J.Kamae

J.Uchi
ZK

J.Kamae

J.Uchi
ZK

Otoshi Uchi
Rei no Ji D

Kesa Uchi
SD

Prepare
KD

Maede Tsuki
SD

Otoshi Uchi
Rei no Ji D

Kesa Uchi
SD

Prepare
KD

Maede Tsuki
SD

Kesa Uchi
SD

(On the spot turn)
ZK

Ura gedan Uchi (Jump turn)

Otoshi Uchi
Rei no Ji D

Kesa Uchi
SD

Naore   RE

UFUGUSUKU NO KUN

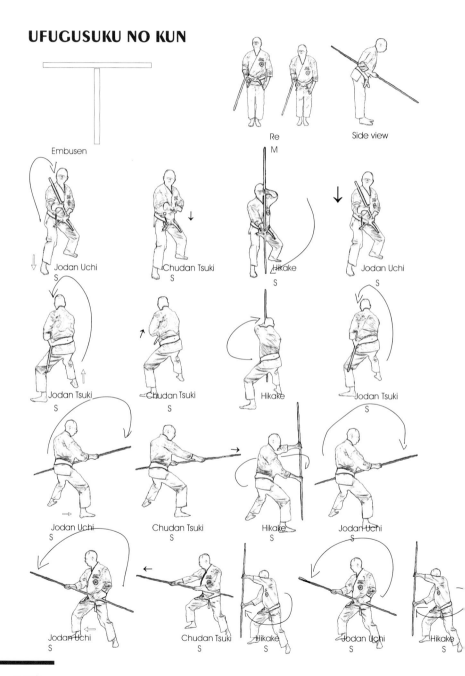

Re
M

Side view

Embusen

Jodan Uchi
S

Chudan Tsuki
S

Hikake
S

Jodan Uchi
S

Jodan Tsuki
S

Chudan Tsuki
S

Hikake

Jodan Tsuki
S

Jodan Uchi
S

Chudan Tsuki
S

Hikake
S

Jodan Uchi
S

Jodan Uchi
S

Chudan Tsuki
S

Hikake
S

Jodan Uchi
S

Hikake
S

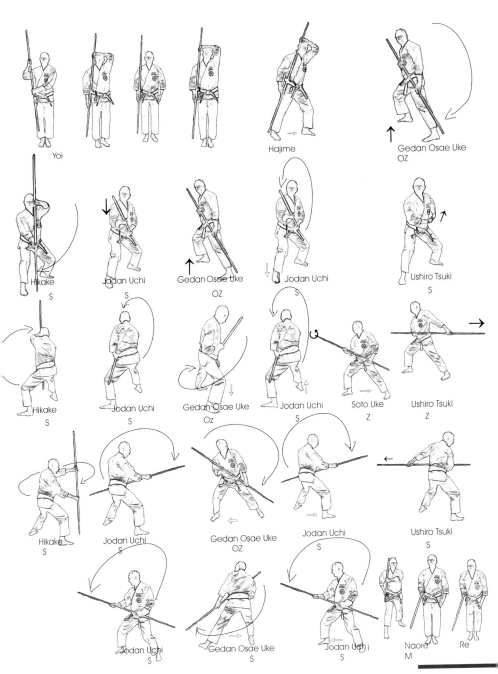

Yoi

Hajime

Gedan Osae Uke
OZ

Hikake
S

Jodan Uchi
S

Gedan Osae Uke
OZ

Jodan Uchi
S

Ushiro Tsuki
S

Hikake
S

Jodan Uchi
S

Gedan Osae Uke
Oz

Jodan Uchi
S

Soto Uke
Z

Ushiro Tsuki
Z

Hikake
S

Jodan Uchi
S

Gedan Osae Uke
OZ

Jodan Uchi
S

Ushiro Tsuki
S

Jodan Uchi
S

Gedan Osae Uke
S

Jodan Uchi
S

Naore
M

Re

OSHIRO NO KUN

Embusen

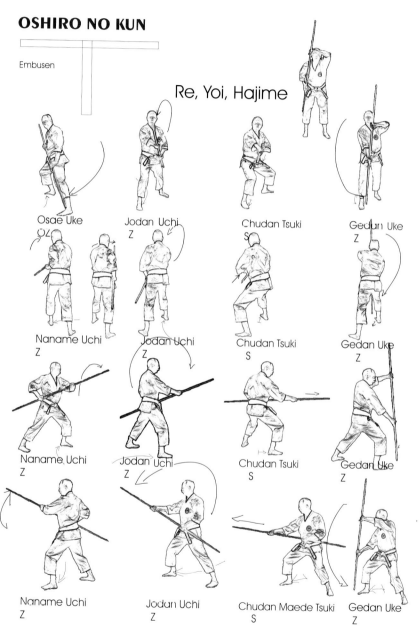

Re, Yoi, Hajime

Osae Uke
OZ

Jodan Uchi
Z

Chudan Tsuki
S

Gedan Uke
Z

Naname Uchi
Z

Jodan Uchi
Z

Chudan Tsuki
S

Gedan Uke
Z

Naname Uchi
Z

Jodan Uchi
Z

Chudan Tsuki
S

Gedan Uke
Z

Naname Uchi
Z

Jodan Uchi
Z

Chudan Maede Tsuki
S

Gedan Uke
Z

Naname Uchi
Z

Jodan Uchi
Z

Osae Uke
OZ

Jodan Uchi
Zk

Ushiro Tsuki

Naname Uchi
Z

Jodan uchi
Z

Osae Uke
OZ

Jodan Uchi
Z

Soto Uke
Z

Ushiro Tsuki
Z

Naname Uchi
Z

Jodan Uchi
Z

Osae Uke
OZ

Jodan Uchi
Z

Ushiro Tsuki
Z

Naname Uchi
Z

Jodan Uchi
Z

Osae Uke
OZ

Jodan Uchi
Z

Naore RE

SUSHI NO KON SHO

Version 1

Embusen

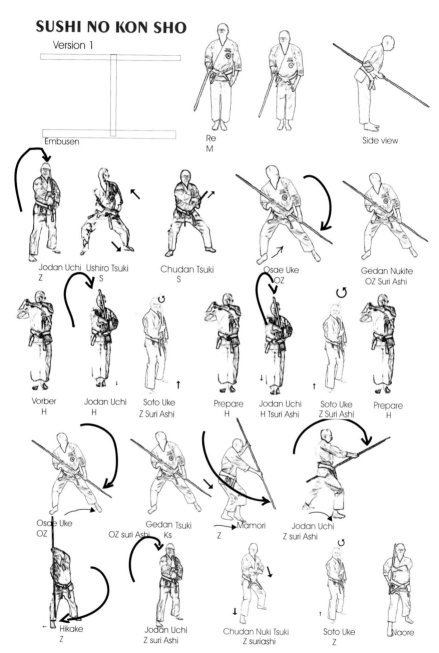

Re
M

Side view

Jodan Uchi Ushiro Tsuki
Z   S

Chudan Tsuki
S

Osae Uke
OZ

Gedan Nukite
OZ Suri Ashi

Vorber
H

Jodan Uchi
H

Soto Uke
Z Suri Ashi

Prepare
H

Jodan Uchi
H Tsuri Ashi

Soto Uke
Z Suri Ashi

Prepare
H

Osae Uke
OZ

Gedan Tsuki
OZ suri Ashi   Ks

Mamori
Z

Jodan Uchi
Z suri Ashi

Hikake
Z

Jodan Uchi
Z suri Ashi

Chudan Nuki Tsuki
Z suriashi

Soto Uke
Z

Naore

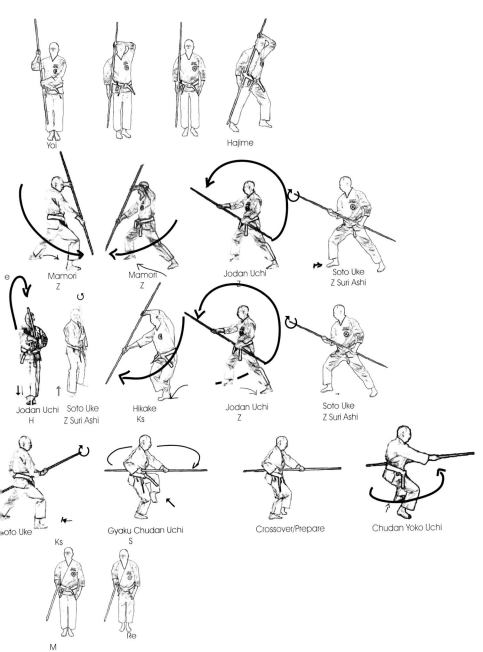

Yoi

Hajime

Mamori
Z

Mamori
Z

Jodan Uchi
Z

Soto Uke
Z Suri Ashi

e

Jodan Uchi
H

Soto Uke
Z Suri Ashi

Hikake
Ks

Jodan Uchi
Z

Soto Uke
Z Suri Ashi

oto Uke
Ks

Gyaku Chudan Uchi
S

Crossover/Prepare

Chudan Yoko Uchi

M

Re

SUSHI NO KON SHO

Version 2

Embusen

Re
M

Side view

Yoi

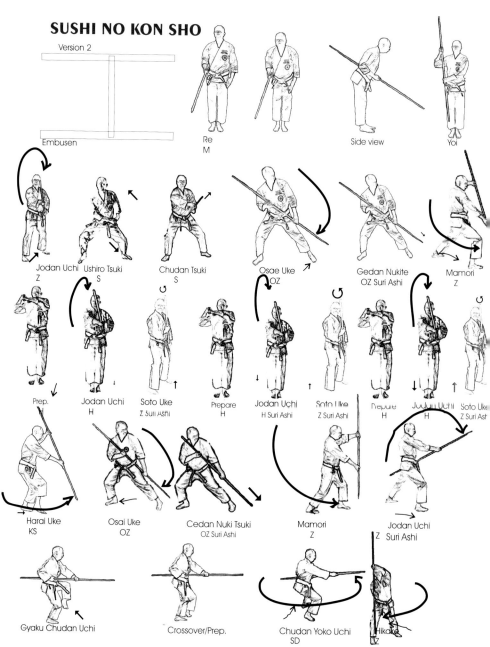

Jodan Uchi
Z

Ushiro Tsuki
S

Chudan Tsuki
S

Osae Uke
OZ

Gedan Nukite
OZ Suri Ashi

Mamori
Z

Prep.

Jodan Uchi
H

Soto Uke
Z Suri Ashi

Prepare
H

Jodan Uchi
H Suri Ashi

Soto Uke
Z Suri Ashi

Prepare
H

Jodan Uchi
H

Soto Uke
Z Suri Ashi

Harai Uke
KS

Osai Uke
OZ

Cedan Nuki Tsuki
OZ Suri Ashi

Mamori
Z

Jodan Uchi
Z Suri Ashi

Gyaku Chudan Uchi

Crossover/Prep.

Chudan Yoko Uchi
SD

Hikake
Z

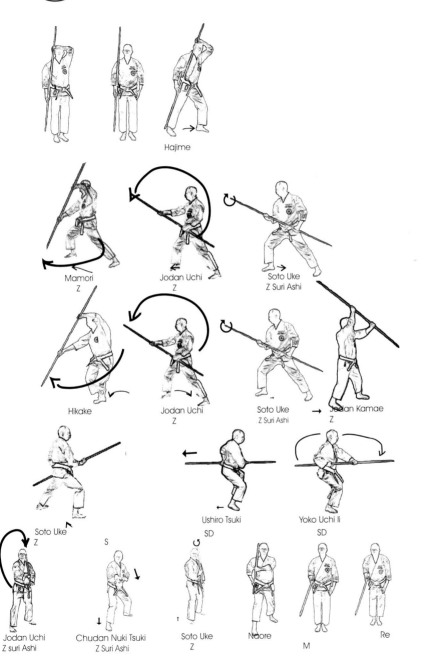

Hajime

Mamori
Z

Jodan Uchi
Z

Soto Uke
Z Suri Ashi

Hikake

Jodan Uchi
Z

Soto Uke
Z Suri Ashi

Jodan Kamae
Z

Soto Uke
Z

Ushiro Tsuki
SD

Yoko Uchi Ii
SD

Jodan Uchi
Z suri Ashi

Chudan Nuki Tsuki
Z Suri Ashi

Soto Uke
Z

Naore
M

Re

SUSHI NO KON SHO

Version 3

Embusen

Hajime

Jodan Uchi
Z

Ushiro Tsuki
S

Morote Tsuki
S

Jodan Uchi
Z

Soto Uke
Z

Pull back

Jodan Uchi
Hs

Soto Uke
Z

Hajime
Hs

Preparation

Pull back
OZ

Gedan Nuki Tsuki
OZ

Gedan Uke
Z

Jodan Uchi
Z

Age Uchi
Z

Osae Uke
OZ

Pull back
OZ

Gedan Nuki Tsuki
OZ

Mamori
Z

Preparation

Jodan Uchi
Z

Soto Uke
Z

Osae Uke
OZ

Pull back
OZ

Nuki Tsuki
OZ

Mamori
Z

Pull back
Z

Shomen Uchi
Z

Nuki Tsuki
Z

Soto Uke
Z

Osae Uke
OZ

Gedan Nuki Tsuki
OZ

Mamori
Z

Hikake
Z

Jodan Uchi
Hs

Soto Uke
Z

Hajime
Hs

Prepare

Jodan Uchi
Hs

Soto Uke
Z

Osae Uke
OZ

Otoshi Uchi
Z

Prepare

Shomen Uchi
Z

Soto Uke
Z

Prepare
OZ

Age Uchi
Z

Otoshi Uchi
Z

Prepare

Shomen Uchi
Z

Ks

Yoko Uchi left
Crossover

Yoko Uchi right
SD

Hikake
Z

Jodan Uchi
Z

Nuki Tsuki
Z

Soto Uke
Z

SUSHI NO KON SHO

Version 4

Embusen

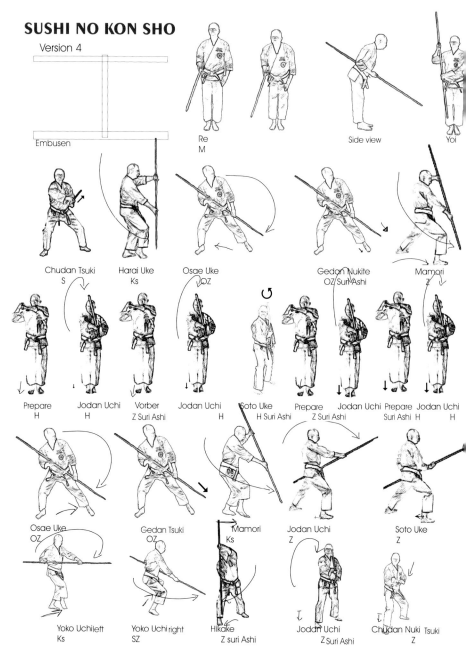

Re
M

Side view

Yoi

Chudan Tsuki
S

Harai Uke
Ks

Osae Uke
OZ

Gedan Nukite
OZ Suri Ashi

Mamori
Z

Prepare
H

Jodan Uchi
H

Vorber
Z Suri Ashi

Jodan Uchi
H

Soto Uke
H Suri Ashi

Prepare
Z Suri Ashi

Jodan Uchi
H

Prepare
Suri Ashi H

Jodan Uchi
H

Osae Uke
OZ

Gedan Tsuki
OZ

Mamori
Ks

Jodan Uchi
Z

Soto Uke
Z

Yoko Uchi left
Ks

Yoko Uchi right
SZ

Hikake
Z suri Ashi

Jodan Uchi
Z Suri Ashi

Chudan Nuki Tsuki
Z

Hajime   Jodan Uchi   Ushiro Tsuki

Mamori
Z

Jodan Uchi
Z

Soto Uke
Z Suri Ashi

Maede Tsuki
Z Tsugi Ashi

Soto Uke
Z Suri Ashi

Hikake
Ks

Jodan Uchi
Z

Soto Uke
Z Suri Ashi

Maede Tsuki
Z Tzugi Ashi

Maede Tsuki
Z

Hikake

Crossover
Ks

Jodan Uch
Z

Age Uchi
Z

Soto Uke
M

Naore

Re

SUSHI NO KUN DAI
Version 1

Embusen

Re   Yoi   Hajime

Mamori
Zk

Jodan Uchi
Zk

Osae Uke
Ozk

Harai Uke
Zk

Osae Uke
Ozk

Harai Uke
Zk

Jodan Uchi
Zk

Soto Uke
Zk

Osae Uke
Ozk

Jodan Uchi
Zk

Soto Uke
Zk

Gyaku Yoko Uchi Chudan
Ks

Gedan Yoko Uchi
SD

Jodan Morote Uke
SD

Gedan Morote Uke
SD

Ura Yoko Uchi
SD

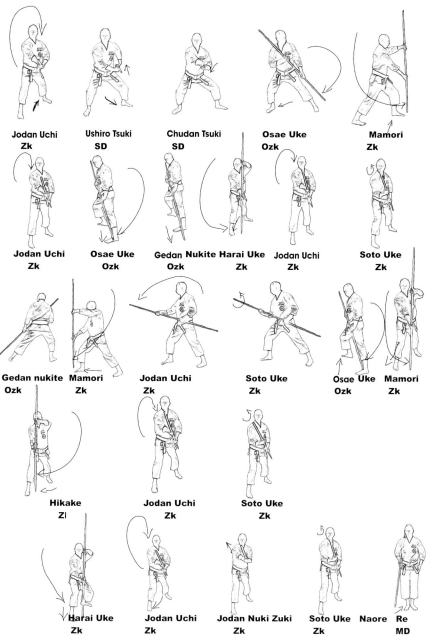

Jodan Uchi Zk	Ushiro Tsuki SD	Chudan Tsuki SD	Osae Uke Ozk	Mamori Zk

Jodan Uchi Zk	Osae Uke Ozk	Gedan Nukite Harai Uke Ozk	Jodan Uchi Zk	Soto Uke Zk

Gedan nukite Ozk	Mamori Zk	Jodan Uchi Zk	Soto Uke Zk	Osae Uke Ozk	Mamori Zk

Hikake ZI	Jodan Uchi Zk	Soto Uke Zk

Harai Uke Zk	Jodan Uchi Zk	Jodan Nuki Zuki Zk	Soto Uke Zk	Naore Re MD

SUSHI NO KUN DAI
Version 2

Embusen

Re Yoi   **Hajime**   **Jodan Uchi**
Zk

Mamori
Zk

Jodan Uchi
Zk

Osae Uke **Nukite** **Harai Uke**
Ozk **Zk**

Osae Uke   **Nukite**   **Harai Uke**   **Jodan Uchi**   **Soto Uke**   **Osae Uke**
Ozk   **Ozk**   **Zk**   **Zk**   **Zk**   **Ozk**

Jodan Uchi   **Soto Uke**   **Gyaku Yoko Uchi Chudan**   **Chudan Yoko Uchi**
Zk   **Zk**   **Ks**   **SD**

Ura Yoko Uchi   **Harai Uke**   **Jodan Uchi**   **Age Uchi** **Otoshi Uchi**
SD   **Zk**   **Zk**   **ZK**

Ushiro Zuki
SD

Chudan Zuki
SD

Osae Uke
Ozk

Osae Uke
Ozk

Mamori
Zk

Jodan Uchi
Zk

Osae Uke
Ozk

Gedan Nukite
Ozk

Harai Uke
Zk

Jodan Uchi
Zk

Soto Uke
Zk

Gedan nukite
Ozk

Mamori
Zk

Jodan Uchi
Zk

Soto Uke
Zk

Osae Uke+Nukite
Ozk

Mamori
Zk

Hikake
ZK

Jodan Uchi
Zk

Soto Uke
Zk

Jodan Morote Uke
SD

Gedan Morote Uke
SD

Jodan Nuki Zuki
Zk

Soto Uke
Zk

Naore

Re
MD

SAKUGAWA NO KON

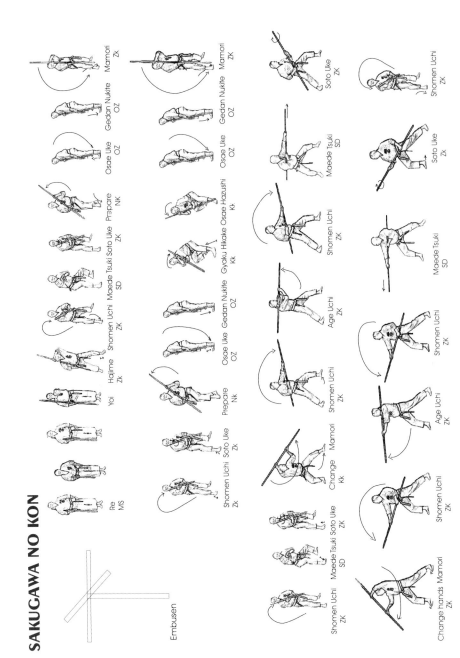

Embusen

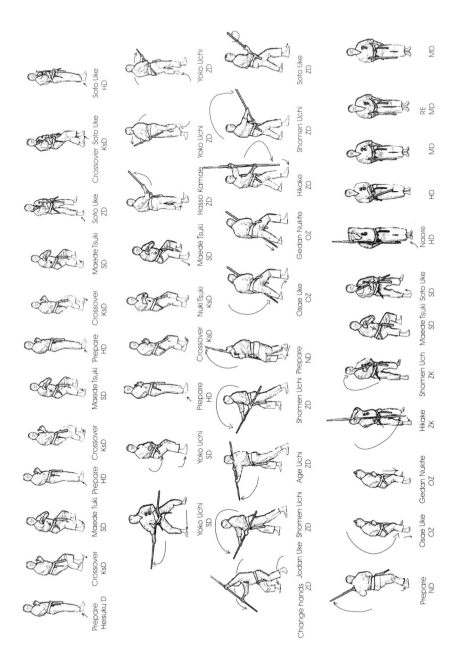

Yoi MS	Hajime SD	Osae Uke Ozk	Shomen Uchi SD	Pull back SD	Chudan Morote Tsuki SD	Hikake SD

Sunakake NkD	Shomen Uchi SD	Pull back SD	Morote Tsuki SD	Hikake SD	Gedan Uke SD

Sunakake NkD	Shomen Uchi SD	Pull back SD	Chudan Morote Tsuki SD	Hikake SD	Gedan Uke SD

Sunakake NkD	Shomen Uchi SD	Pull back SD	Chudan Morote Tsuki SD	Hikake SD	Gedan Uke SD

Naore	Yoi	Re

Embusen

Gedan Uke SD	Shomen Uchi SD	Sunakake SD	Osae Uke Ozk	Shomen Uchi ZD	Ushiro Tsuki ZD
Shomen Uchi SD	Sunakake SD	Osae Uke Ozk	Shomen Uchi Zk	Soto Uke Zk ZK	Ushiro Tsuki 90° Rotating
Shomen Uchi SD	Sunakake SD	Osae Uke Ozk	Shomen Uchi Zk	Ushiro Tsuki ZK	
Shomen Uchi SD	Sunakake SD	Osae Uke Ozk	Shomen Uchi ZK **Kiai**		

UFUGUSUKU NO KUN

Version 2

BUNKAI Ufugusuku No Kun 2

Osae Uke / Gedan Nukite

Shomen Uchi / Moroto Uke

Gedan Uke / Gedan Uchi

Shomen Uchi / Moroto Uke

Shomen Uchi / Moroto Uke

Naore

3 Yoi

4 Hajime

7 Morote Tsuki / Gyaku Hikake

8 Hikake / Moroto Tsuki

11 Sunakake / Morote Tsuki

12 Osae Uke / Gedan Tsuki

15 RE

16

KUMI BO ICHI (1)

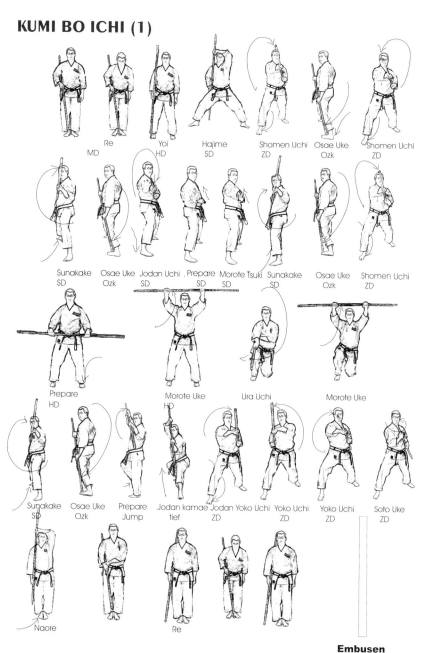

Re
MD

Yoi
HD

Hajime
SD

Shomen Uchi
ZD

Osae Uke
Ozk

Shomen Uchi
ZD

Sunakake
SD

Osae Uke
Ozk

Jodan Uchi
SD

Prepare
SD

Morote Tsuki
SD

Sunakake
SD

Osae Uke
Ozk

Shomen Uchi
ZD

Prepare
HD

Morote Uke
HD

Ura Uchi

Morote Uke

Sunakake
SD

Osae Uke
Ozk

Prepare
Jump

Jodan kamae
tief

Jodan Yoko Uchi
ZD

Yoko Uchi
ZD

Yoko Uchi
ZD

Soto Uke
ZD

Naore

Re

Embusen

BUNKAI KUMI BO I

RE

Hajime

Shomen Uchi / Morote Uke

Osae Uke / Gedan Nukite

Shomen Uchi / Shomen Uchi

Morote Tsuki/Morote Tsuki

Sunakake/Sunakake

Osae Uke/Gedan Nukite

Jodan Uchi/Morote Uke

Morote Uke/Shomen Uchi

Ura Uchi/Jump

Morote Uke/Shomen Uchi

Sunakake/Sunakake

Osae Uke/Gedan Nukite

Prepare to jump back

Jodan Uke both jump back

Jodan Yoko (Men) Uchi both

Gyaku Jodan Yoko Uchi both

Jodan Yoko Uchi

Soto Uke both

Naore

Yoi

Yoi

CONCLUDING REMARKS

Kobudo (formerly called Kobu-Jutsu) uses a great number of different weapons. Whereas a great number of Katas could be passed on to Bo-Jutsu, the same thing has only been achieved for different weapons in a restricted way. In addition to martial arts without weapons (Karate, Aikido, Jujutsu and others) Kobudo is being practiced at almost every school. As practicing with weapons often demands total concentration, it is advisable, especially for beginners, to start their training program with weapons and to continue without weapons afterwards.

As a matter of principle, before the students can be introduced to the Kobudo techniques, they should have the important basic techniques of the martial arts without weapons under control. As a rule, the long stick (Bo) is the basic weapon for Kobudo. The other weapons, such as Tonfa, Nunchaku, Sai and Kama, make higher demands on the students. That does not only apply to movements but also to the risk of injury.

However, every experienced martial arts fighter knows that practicing with weapons serves to improve and to support the techniques of martial arts without weapons, as for example the sense of motion in Karate. The techniques of martial arts with empty hands become more exact and quicker. Insofar, Kobudo is not only a welcome supplement but even more an essential enlargement of the martial arts practiced so far. On the one hand, the main task of future Great Masters will be to preserve the knowledge about the martial arts steeped in tradition, on the other hand, they must also develop different techniques of the weapons further.

The IMAF-Kokusai Budoin (International Martial Art Federation) is a non-profit organization overseeing the different Budo disciplines. It was founded after World War II in 1952. In February 1952 the first Budo Exhibition was presented in the Hibiya Park in Tokyo. The first Budo demonstration was planned in 1951 by K. Mifune, K. Ito and S. Sato (Judo), H. Nakayama and H. Takano (Kendo), H. Otsuka (Karate), K. Wake and S. Kiyura. Prince Tsunenori Kaya was elected the first president of the National Japan Health Association, the original name of the IMAF. The present president is Yasuhisa Tokugawa, a member of the ancient Tokugawa Dynasty, a family of Shoguns who ruled in Japan in peace for nearly 300 years. The IMAF has seven Departments: Judo, Kendo, Karatedo, Iaido, Aikido, Nihon Jujutsu and Kobudo. In these departments there are different styles of martial arts. The IMAF is inaugurated by the family of the Tenno to give high ranks in all kinds of Budo art and to give titles of honor (Renshi, Kyoshi, Hanshi, and Mejin). Since its foundation, the aim of the IMAF Kokusai Budoin has been to make Japanese Martial Arts popular in the whole world and seek for further development.

The vision is that with the help of Budo arts all people in the world learn how to live in harmony. It aims to help them work for peace and understanding between different nations. The IMAF Kokusai Budoin has members in more than 50 nations, 17 branch directors are responsible for international exchange. The IMAF has friendly relations to other Budo organisations; some leaders are honorary members of the IMAF.

Contact:	Fax	E-Mail	E-Info
International			www.imaf.net
IMAF Japan	81-42-566-4425	sato@imafwdhq.gol.com	
IMAF			
Chairman Europe:	049-7661-99132	h.-d.rauscher@imaf-germany.de	www.imaf-germany.de
H.-D. Rauscher			
IMAF Chairman USA:			
Bret Mayfield	(082)-295-9079	vtimaf@aol.com	www.imafusa.com
Tetsuhiro Hokama	(089)945-6148	address: 147-2 Uehara Nishihara, Okinawa 903-0125, Japan	

I am particularly grateful to my students and my two sons for their support in planning the book and their assistance during the photo sessions. Their names are listed in the acknowledgments that follow the text. Thanks also to my wife Elvira for her patience and for taking the numerous photos. Thanks to my friend Horst Steur Ph.D. for the English translation of the German original. Thanks also to Meyer & Meyer Sport, especially to Miss Dalley, Mrs. Deutz, Mr. Stengel and Mr. Lundszien. They realized an excellent design and presentation for this book.

Lutz Kogel
3. Dan Shotokan Karate

Marc Kogel
2. Dan Shotokan Karate

Klaus Parensen
1. Dan Shotokan Karate

Phillipp Hans
1. Kyu Shotokan Karate

LITERATURE

Books/Journals

Clavell, J. (1988). *Sunzi – Die Kunst des Krieges.* Droemersche Verlagsanstalt Th.Knaur Nachf., München: Verlagsanstalt Th. Knaur.

Demura, F. (1976). *Bo – Karate weapon of self defense.* Ohara Publications incorporated.

Garelli, A. (2002). *Bo – Kampf mit dem Langstock.* Verl. Weimann Berlin 1. Aufl.

Hokama, T. (1996). *Okinawan Karate.* Masters Publication Hamilton, Ontario, Kanada.

Inoue, M. (1987). *Bo, Sai, Tonfa and Nunchaku – Ancient Martial Art of the Ryukyu Islands.* Japan Publications Seitohsha Co, Ltd.

Jakhel, R. (1997). *Modernes Sport-Karate.* Aachen: Meyer & Meyer Verlag.

Kogel, H. (2003). *50 Jahre IMAF Kokusai Budoin.* Budoworld IMAF Special Okt. 2003, 5-8.

Kogel, H. (2001). Relationship between Budo and Medicine. In: *Ido – Movement for Culture.* Vol. 3, Ass. Idokan Poland. Rzeszów.

Kogel, H. (2003). 50 Jahre IMAF-Kokusai Budoin – Das alljapanische Martial Arts Festival in Tokyo. *Budoworld, 28* (6), 42-45.

Kogel, H. (2003). 50 Jahre IMAF Kokusai Budoin. *Budoworld Karate, 28* (1), 82-86.

Kogel, H. (2004). Okinawa Kobudo – Zurück zu den Wurzeln. *Budoworld, 29* (6), 14-18.

Lind, W. (1997). *Okinawa Karate.* Berlin: Sportverlag.

Mc Carthy, P. (1995). *The bible of karate – bubishi.* Tuttle Publishing Boston, Rutlat, VT, Tokyo.

Mc Carthy, P. (1999). *Ancient Okinawan martial arts – koryu uchinada.* Tuttle Publishing Boston, Rutland, VT, Tokyo.

Musashi, M. (2002). *Fünf Ringe.* München: Droemersche Verlagsanstalt Th. Knaur Nachf.

Presas, R. (1983). *Modern Arnis.* Ohara Publications Inc.

Stiebler, G. (1994). *Bo-Karate, Hanbo-Jitsu.* Niederhausen: Falken Verlag.

Videos

Hokama, T. (1992). *Bo-Jutsu.* Mastersline Video Publ. Inc.

Matayoshi, S. (1995). *Kobudo – The weapon arts of Okinawa.* Tsunami Productions.

Oshiro, T. (1996). *Yamanni ryu – Okinawan bo-jutsu.* Tsunami Productions 1996.

Shinzato, Y. (2002) *Okinawa kobudo.* Budo Intern. Publ. Co.

Photo & Illustration Credits

Cover photo und inside photos: Elvira Kogel
Illustrations: Helmut Kogel
Cover design: Jens Vogelsang